MsMarmiteLover's SECRET TEA PARTY

Kerstin Rodgers

◨ SQUARE PEG

This book is dedicated to my daughter, Sienna Poppy Carmela,
who has now left home for university, and to all empty–nest mums.

Introduction

If you want to entertain, tea, as in an afternoon tea party, is a cheaper, more manageable meal to prepare than dinner. Another advantage is that the majority of this meal can be made beforehand, enabling the host or hostess to sit with their guests.

Tea can be as simple as a drink and a biscuit, but afternoon tea is at its most glorious, and most British, when it becomes a small feast, with good baking, hot drinks and a little tipple or two. Realistically, unless you are a lady who lunches, with a retinue of servants, occasions such as afternoon tea parties are reserved for the weekends, when you have time to bake, time to dress up, time to decorate the room and table, time to enjoy.

Tea is a meal at which, above all, you eat with your eyes. Prettiness is essential. A cake is like a fashion accessory: a Birkin bag, a fascinator, or a pair of soft leather Italian gloves. Not necessary, perhaps, but very covetable.

You don't have to be hungry to enjoy an afternoon tea. Real life is on hold. Food as fuel is notionally cast away. It can be playful; even as an adult you can revert to the simple childhood pleasure of jam sandwiches.

Four o'clock is the time of day when our Circadian rhythms are at their lowest. We need that blood sugar boost. At work, the tea or coffee break is enshrined in law: employers recognise that we work harder when we are sufficiently hydrated.

Tea is a moment to wear Sunday best, get out the best china, play a character from a period drama such as *Upstairs, Downstairs*, *Peaky Blinders* or *Miss Marple*. We hunger for elaborate formality in a casual, dress-down world. If you have a liking for vintage clothes, tea is a time when it's perfectly acceptable in the 21st century to wear hats and gloves, stockings or fake fur stoles; to sit up straight, perhaps with the aid of a corset, and indulge in small talk, although you may also debate feminism, politics, the environment, home educating, conspiracy theories... I've had guests covered in tattoos doing their knitting between courses, reminiscent of *les tricoteuses* at the guillotine.

Tea is also a repast associated with gossip: 'Love and scandal are the best sweeteners of tea', said the writer Henry Fielding. Cultivate your best stories, buff up your anecdotes, polish your putdowns and channel Maggie Smith, the acid-tongued Dowager Countess of Downton Abbey, for an afternoon tea party should be laced with decorum and dirty linen.

The tea hour came about in the 18th century, when the upper classes, who could afford candles and gaslight in the evenings, took their 'dinner' between 11a.m. and noon, while 'supper' was between 7 and 8.30p.m. That is a rather long time to be without food. Tea evolved from a refreshing drink to a small mid-afternoon meal that would keep you going until the evening.

The Duchess of Bedford is generally considered to be the pioneer of the British afternoon tea party. In her day it was not so much ladies who lunched, as ladies who took tea. Tea was considered a feminine drink, taken in the private boudoir or bedroom of a lady. Even today the hostess serves tea, pouring from the pot: 'Shall I be mother?' goes the cliché.

What with the Duchess of Bedford inventing teatime and the Earl of Sandwich inventing sandwiches, no wonder afternoon tea tends to be an occasion where everyone pretends to be an aristocrat. The food for a tea was always delicate, fit for refined ladies with bird-like appetites, although bread was a key element, with finger sandwiches and sweet biscuits. Gradually, as the grand hotels took to marketing their own afternoon teas, the meal grew bigger.

Even within the 'afternoon tea' format there are different types:

- A 'cream tea' involves scones or splits and cream, probably clotted. This is a contest between neighbouring English counties, Devon v Cornwall.
- A 'low tea' was so called because it was taken at low tables, such as card or coffee tables.
- A 'high tea' is served at a proper dining table with chairs.

There are north/south differences too. In the north, 'tea' is dinner and 'dinner' is lunch. The working-class habit was to have a substantial breakfast, a large midday dinner and a light snack before bed. The more rural north of England (and French) farmers still eat this way. By contrast the aristocracy and urban classes of the south ate a large breakfast, a lighter lunch, an afternoon tea and a late dinner.

While I feature unusual sweet recipes and styling tips in this book, I retain a decent proportion of savoury recipes. A successful afternoon tea needs the contrast between salty and sweet, otherwise it's a mawkish sugar overload. When I host secret teas, I confess it's mostly women and gay men that book. Straight men prefer savouries, we are led to believe. Is afternoon tea the meal that dare not speak its name?

In this age of equality, it is interesting how food is still gendered. Perhaps because afternoon tea is rather a frivolous occasion, a chance to prettify the table, the room, the outfits and the cooking, it tends to appeal to women more than men. Brunches on the other hand, attract more men. Tea is for ladies, coffee is for guys. Cake is for girls, meat is for men. The exception to this gendering occurs north of Watford: it seems that northern men are confident and metrosexual enough to enjoy cake in public! *The Great British Bake-Off* has had several male winners, so it's clear that men love to bake and that men love cake.

An essential element of afternoon tea is baked goods. Baking, like knitting, has long been a touchstone of 'good' motherhood. (Even though I can't knit, I felt that I couldn't be a good mother unless I tackled needles and wool while pregnant. I eventually managed a plain knit 'waistcoat', full of holes, three sizes too big for my baby girl).

Nigella Lawson brilliantly tapped into the postmodern feminist desire to spend time, baking, in the kitchen, with her 2000 publication *How to Be a Domestic Goddess: Baking and the Art of Comfort Cooking*. The iconic cover, adorned with a small, singular cake, glossed with low-rise white icing and topped with a sugar-craft rose, spoke to all of us, me included, who learnt to bake at nursery school and yearned to reproduce that comforting shared moment with our own children.

This return to the skills of yesteryear (but no hectoring tone, it's a choice, we must be realistic and pragmatic: modern women's lives are different) has been reflected also by the success on TV of shows such as *The Great British Bake-Off* and *The Sewing Bee*.

Baking from scratch is once again popular. The urge to bake and master that process is in part a reaction to a world in which high streets increasingly look the same. People long for individuality, for the handmade, for original one-off creations. Crafting and cooking food has links to 'austerity chic' and the desire of working women, who do not have the time to be 'proper' full-time home-makers, to fulfil that basic nesting urge. This book inspires people to embark on projects of varying difficulty and commitment.

My baking talents had long been dormant, but were resuscitated for the decade ahead with the obligatory annual birthday cake for my daughter. Every mother, no matter how high-powered her job or how many hours a day she works, secretly yearns to be Ma Walton, and the odd Sunday spent donning an apron and baking a cake, soothes and calms that nagging feeling of not being 'good enough'. In America, sweethearts and mothers send cakes in jars – to protect the cakes from damage – to their sons serving in Iraq and Afghanistan. Baking a cake is almost a cliché of motherly love, sugar and spice and all things nice.

Tea is also the favourite meal of children, encompassing as it does feelings of comfort, nurture and sheer fun. The ritual of coming home from school, offloading worries about teachers and friends to mum, learning to cook by osmosis while sitting in the kitchen – these form the memories of childhood. My own introduction to cooking was via chocolate butterfly cakes, a class taught at nursery school. I was impressed that we had learnt how to make our own sweet things, and by the fantasy element: here was a cake that, by the simple expedient of slicing off the top, cutting it in half and plunging the halves into buttercream, formed the spongy wings of a butterfly!

I must admit, I wasn't a very good cake-maker, to the point that my daughter would plead with me yearly, her birthday looming, when I'd roll up my sleeves and have another go, to buy a shop-bought cake. The purchase of a decent oven in 2008 changed all that: it wasn't me, it was my oven!

Since I bought a decent oven, my baking skills have gone from strength to strength. I hosted the first 'Underground Tea' in my living room in April 2009 and, since then, several secret tea rooms have sprung up around the country, some of which have provided guest recipes for this book. There are many reasons for this popularity: the enduring and simple appeal of cake; the baking boom; and the fact that tea is often seen as a safer, more manageable option than a supper club for a lone female hostess.

An offshoot of secret tea rooms is the cake club, where people bring along home-baked cakes to clubs at various locations. The bakers, for the most part women, eye each other's creations beadily. One such club has a strict, if rather arcane, rule: NO cupcakes. The traditional large cake is favoured. But sometimes a small cake, demonstrating perfect portion control, is what is needed. Cupcakes are sneered at by some and blamed for muscling out the less flashy English fairy cake. But I must avow a liking for the gaudy, exuberant, top-heavy cupcake, the Liberace of baking. I'm an equal ops baker, no petty prejudices here.

At the back of this book is a list of secret tea rooms around the country where you can experience the best of British baking in people's homes (see page 248).

1. Dressing the Table

When entertaining, I always feel calmer once the table is laid, providing the frame for the picture-perfect meal to come. A beautifully set table is a treat for the eyes, and for afternoon tea, beauty is imperative. Vintage china can be bought very cheaply at car boot sales, a few sprigs of wildflowers look pretty in a bottle, while a vintage tea towel or 'fat quarter' can be transformed into a serviette. The point is: you don't need much money to create something stylish. Unless you have a particularly lovely table, use a tablecloth (I've even used old linen bed sheets). But plain or patterned (matte, not shiny) wrapping paper or banqueting roll will also do. This chapter is about the art of the table, what goes under the food rather than in it.

Furnishing the Table

Napkins

Ever been on a cruise? The staff are trained to shape your towels into animals such as dolphins, cranes and monkeys, which they leave on your bed. When I talk about the language of napkins, I'm not exhorting you to learn some form of textile origami, this is clearly for the host who has time on their hands, but it is worthwhile thinking how best to place a napkin on the table. Traditionally the napkin goes on the left, to the side of the last fork. You can also use a napkin ring. Other placements include a fan shape, concertina style, in the middle, or sprouting out of a glass.

The word 'napkin' comes from the French *nappe* tablecloth, or *napper* to cover. According to Nancy Mitford, populariser of the U (chic) and non-U (not chic) lists of English usage, posh people say 'napkin'. Napkin is U and serviette is non-U. Americans never say 'serviette': that would smack of pretension. Personally I'm quite partial to pretension.

Old textbooks talk about the different napkin shapes: the casket, the cardinal's hat, the lily, water lily, pyramid, and the slightly gynaecological 'collegiate'. There are dozens. Here are four main ones with illustrations. Have fun!

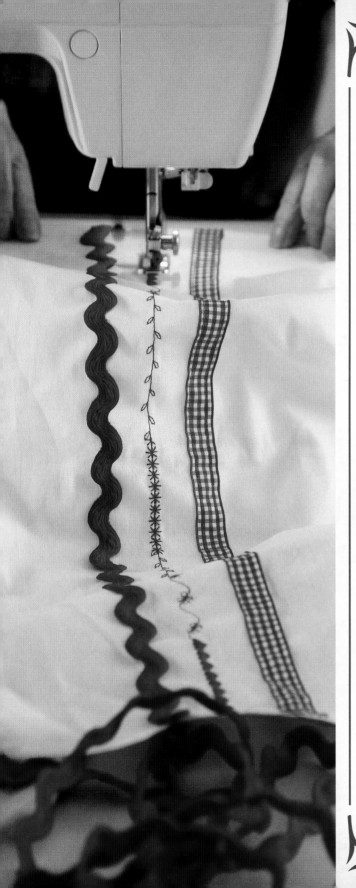

Make Your Own Tea Towels

On my frequent sojourns to France, I always keep a beady eye out for old linen, particularly linen tea towels with the characteristic red stripe down the side. They usually cost between £5 and £10, which is expensive, but they are long-lasting and, with no fluffy bits, are great for drying glasses.

You can make your own tea towels by buying tea towel blanks online (if you are going to the effort, invest in linen – see stockists on page 250) or by stitching fabric in rectangles. If you don't have a sewing machine or feel unconfident with a needle and thread, use an iron-on adhesive.

Make sure you wash the fabric before sewing on to it. You want it pre-shrunk so that the design doesn't buckle. A tea towel is an item that will be washed a great deal, after all.

Here are some ideas, which can of course be applied to napkins too. Have a go, those gorgeous but expensive tea towels you covet in designer shops are yours to create now!

- Sew a length of ribbon or ric rac braid (preferably cotton) to either end of the tea towel, leaving a plain border of about 3cm. If you have a sewing machine, experiment with the embroidery settings: I did a series of hearts, crosses, flowers and leaves that look very pretty.
- You can also stitch three coloured lines (nice in red or pink) along the ends to imitate old-fashioned French tea towels.
- Cut out a fabric appliqué and either sew (using a 'satin' stitch) or iron it on.
- Add trimming, such as sturdy lace borders, to each end.

Placemats

During my childhood we always ate dinner on thick, felt-backed scenes of Westminster. A bit grim, Big Ben looming under your supper. Another classic table mat option is one made with raffia, which is good for a trattoria look if that's what you are going for.

I suggest you design your own placemat, perhaps using a favourite drawing, or a knife and fork, or your logo, including the menu of your afternoon tea so that your guests can take them home as souvenirs. Alternatively, laminate a magazine page or a piece of floral wallpaper so that you can wipe them down after use.

Coasters

I loathe coasters; I think they lead to accidents. Maybe it's an age thing. My mum insists on having a coaster under every drink. You live in fear of mistakenly putting your cup of tea down anywhere without the prophylactic underneath. Better to get a table that doesn't stain. But you may possess a French-polished mahogany antique dining table with a magnificent shine. In which case, you may want a coaster.

Doilies

You may think doilies are overly girly, but a nice bit of crochet and afternoon tea are a classic 'marriage' in table-decorating convention. You can get coloured doilies or floral ones in paper that can pull together a cake collection by being placed on top of each plate. I use the word 'collection' with intent. Dressing a table is a form of fashion, with the added bonus of not having to worry about how fat you are and whether you can fit into anything.

Table Runners

I've never been a fan of a long strip of cloth running down the middle of a table, I'm just not that fussy. But don't let that hold you back. It's basically the little sister to the full-blown tablecloth. Make sure your table runner is longer than the table and hangs down equally at both ends. It should be a third of the width of the table.

Or you can also use several table runners placed across the width of the table.

Tablecloths

If you are buying or making a tablecloth, measure the width and length of your table, then add 15–25cm all the way round so that you get the correct amount of drop on each side. Tablecloths traditionally hang 10–20cm from the table.

The best linen is from Belfast. You can't go wrong with a white tablecloth. (I used to refuse to go into restaurants with pink tablecloths, I felt that it was a sign that they didn't take their food seriously. I realise that was harsh and irrational.) I'm also a fan of the chequered tablecloth, in cheery red and white for picnics. The Mexican oilcloth comes in many garish and in-your-face patterns, but these are possibly more appropriate for lunch than tea, depending on your theme.

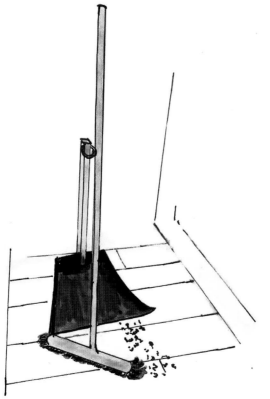

Laundry and Household Tips

Cleaning

Remove candle wax stains by placing a couple of squares of kitchen paper over the stain and ironing it using a medium heat. The wax will melt and the oily stain will be absorbed into the paper.

If you live in a hard-water area such as London, use a couple of tablespoons of bicarbonate of soda to stop limescale forming in your washing machine. Use diluted vinegar overnight to descale your kettle.

Starch

You can buy starch in boxes, which is cheaper than spray cans. After doing your laundry, soak the tablecloths in the diluted starch, then spin dry and hang. Iron while still slightly damp. The great thing about starch is that stains are washed out along with the starch.

Scent

Create a scented tablecloth by spraying it with rose or orange-blossom water when you are ironing the cloth.

Tea for Cleaning

Tea leaves have historically been used to clean and sterilise. Hospital wards were swept with tea leaves.

Mrs Rundell mentions this is the 'directions to servants' chapter in her book *A New System of Domestic Cookery* (published 1806):

To Dust Carpets and Floors.
Sprinkle tea leaves on them, then sweep carefully.
The former should not be swept frequently.

Setting the Table

Charger Plates

Sometimes you just want an opportunity to get out all your lovely china. Charger plates are the larger plates that sit underneath the plate from which you eat. They are often in an accent colour. When laying a table you've got to balance two things: wanting as little washing up as you can get away with and desiring to make it look as pretty as possible.

Tea Sets

Tea sets became popular in Victorian times, when tea drinking moved from being the exclusive province of the wealthy and aristocratic to a popular middle-class pastime.

Cup and Saucer or Mug?

I remember my nan drinking tea from the saucer. I rather like that. Granny chic. Mugs are less washing up, but science has proven that the container you drink or eat from does affect its taste. Drinking from porcelain fine bone china is a special treat.

Collecting

The afternoon tea party appeals to those of us who like to collect homeware or kitchenware. I've been amassing blue-and-white willow patterned china for over a decade, I'm now expanding into green, brown and pink willow. I've also got a good collection of cut glassware. I have a friend, Aoife Behan, who runs pop-ups in Edinburgh (Jelly & Gin) and collects utilityware, subtle pastel-shaded china from the Second World War. Another friend, Rachelle Blondel from The Secret Teacup in Yorkshire, collects vintage Pyrex with milky glass and turquoise wheatsheafs. I tend to get little obsessions and start collecting. No wonder I have no room. But, if you have afternoon teas, you have an excuse for collecting wonderful china!

Basic Tea Set-up

Small plates, in the centre.

Napkins, left of plate.
Etiquette note: if you leave the table, place the napkin on your chair.

Cake fork, left of plate, either on napkin or to the right of it.
(In the USA, the tines are up, in the UK, the tines are down.)

Knife, right of plate, sharp side pointing towards the plate.

Butter knife, right of knife, again sharp side pointing towards the plate.

Spoon, right of knives.

Teaspoon, above right of spoons; can also be placed on the saucer of the teacup.
Etiquette note: Do not place silverware on the tablecloth once used, replace on the saucer or plate.

Teacup and saucer, right of spoons.
Etiquette note: you only lift the cup, not the saucer, unless you are standing up.

Teapots

'Teapots should be china or earthenware.'
George Orwell

The classic teapot in the UK came about in the late 18th century after tax on tea was reduced to the point that everybody could afford to drink it. Originally teapots were teeny, often imported from China, as tea was very expensive and loose. They were rarely washed as the clay would become saturated with the built-up flavour of the tea. Early teapots looked more like coffee pots, but people soon realised that the tea wasn't mixing properly – the hot water remained at the top while the tea leaves sank to the bottom, so the style evolved to today's bowl shape. There are also pear-shaped and oblong pots. In the UK, Joseph Wedgwood produced elegant but mass-produced porcelain china tea sets. The Brown Betty, made from a red clay from Stoke-on-Trent, retained the heat effectively and was popular in the early 20th century. Today teapots, although rarely used, are bigger, to fit in tea bags. I'm a fan of glass teapots when using pretty or speciality teas.

Tea Strainers

If you are using leaf tea, you will need one of these. They are very useful objects also for dusting small amounts of icing sugar or cocoa powder on to baked goods.

Tea Cosies

These keep the teapot warm. They can be knitted or sewn from material. Nowadays we have central heating and mostly use them for effect rather than insulation.

Teaspoons

Sometimes you feel you are fighting a losing battle. As cookery writers we spend hours developing simple recipes, trying to encourage people to cook. My daughter has grown up with me cooking from scratch. But the other day when I asked her to pass me a teaspoon, she furrowed her pretty little nineteen-year-old brow and said, 'Wait, that's the small spoon isn't it?'. I despair.

In America they call them coffee spoons. Weird, huh?

Fortune-telling: Reading the Tea Leaves

Professor Trelawney, played marvellously as a goggle-eyed, batty eccentric by Emma Thompson in the Harry Potter films, read the tea leaves, a skill called, variously, tessomancy, tesseography or tasseomancy, words derived from the French for 'teacup', *tasse*. It is best to use a teacup that is light coloured on the inside, with no distracting patterns. Obviously only loose tea can be used, preferably with larger leaves rather than small bits.

Place the tea leaves inside the teacup and pour boiling water three-quarters of the way up the inside of the cup. Bubbles are a sign of fortune. Tea leaves bobbing on the surface mean that guests could be arriving soon. Spilling a little tea while stirring is good luck.

The guest should drink the tea, sipping it slowly, while you chat. If the guest is right-handed, have them lift the cup and drink with their left hand, and vice versa.

When there is only a little puddle of tea left in the cup, take it from the guest and swirl it clockwise seven times.

Placing a napkin over the saucer, quickly turn the cup over and on to the napkin, leaving it there for a count of three, then turn the cup the right side up.

The handle of the teacup should be facing towards the reader.

Start the reading, clockwise, from the top of the cup, around the rim, which represents the near future. The middle section of the cup represents the future and the bottom, the distant future.

As the 'diviner', let your mind relax and roam, interpret the symbols as you see fit. The more you practise, the more confident you will feel. Be responsible with your fortune telling, don't use this as an opportunity to tell your friend the things that irritate you about her or your opinion on how badly she is running her life. Let your unconscious stream an interpretation of the symbols you see.

- MONEY
- ring – endings completion marriage
- snake movement - travel, water
- BIRD SHAPE journey travel - aircraft
- Diamond Fortunate
- oblong - illness
- series of events
- problems
- Flower shape happiness
- cup - celebration baby
- romance
- mother be receptive
- yes. right direction
- No. wrong direction
- stop
- wheel means progress
- home anchor shape

Final Flourishes

Flowers

Flowers, along with candles, really add to the glamour of afternoon tea.

You don't really want large displays of flowers on the table as people would like to be able to talk to one another, rather than around a plant. I often use wild flowers from my 'secret garden'.

Tea roses are a lovely choice, the name derives from their fragrance of Chinese black tea, as well as their rumoured parentage, a hybrid of Chinese roses. The tea rose is the classic rose shape, with furled petals. They aren't very hardy in a cold climate so are bred with other roses to make the modern 'hybrid Tea Rose'.

Tips

- Cut the stems at a 45° angle with sharp scissors.
- Strip any leaves from the base of each stem.
- A crushed aspirin in the water will keep flowers longer.
- Use vintage jam jars, tea cups, milk jugs or sugar bowls as mini flower vases.

The language of flowers is called 'floriography'; this was particularly popular during Victorian times. 'Talking' bouquets known as nosegays or tussie-mussies, were used for covert communication. Below are a few examples from Kate Greenaway's 1884 illustrated book *The Language of Flowers*:

Bluebells	Constancy
Carnations, yellow	Disdain
Carnations, striped	Refusal
Chrysanthemum, red	I love
Chrysanthemum, white	Truth
Chrysanthemum, yellow	Slighted love
Crocus, saffron	Mirth
Daisy	Innocence
French marigold	Jealousy
Day lily	Coquetry

And while the rose generally means Love, each colour has a specific message. Rose, York and Lancaster means War while Rose, White and Red together means Unity. A full blown rose placed over two buds signifies Secrecy.

Make Your Own Cake Stand

I love cake stands but they can be pricey. Here is an easy way to make your own. It works well with cut glass that might look a bit tacky as separate pieces. Or you could use china candlesticks that are perhaps a bit modern, with a vintage china plate.

You will need:

Candlestick
Glass/ceramic glue
Nice plate

Clean and dry the plate and candlestick. Find the centre of the plate and mark the spot. Prepare the glue according to packet instructions, then turn your plate upside down and apply a thin coat to the centre of the bottom of your plate using a brush or stick. Don't touch the glue with your bare hands.

Place the top of the candlestick in the gluey centre of the bottom of the plate. Work quickly because the glue dries fast. While the glue is still tacky, remove any excess with a paper towel and nail polish remover.

To make a tiered cake stand, do the same again, with a smaller candlestick and plate on top.

Place a heavy book on top to hold the base down and leave it to dry overnight. These cake stands are not dishwasher-safe, so gently wash them by hand.

Make Your Own Teacup Candles

Did you know that those small 'tea light' candles are so-called because they were originally devised for warming teapots?

Candles are a byword for romance and prettiness. Ladies of a certain age preferred tall candles that would cast a flattering light at the dining table, rather than low ones that would light from below and leave one looking like something from a horror film. Even during the day it's glamorous to have a few starry points of waxy light. For the teacups, use vintage crockery found at car boot sales and charity shops. The other supplies can be bought online from specialist candle suppliers.

Allow about 200ml of wax per teacup (the average teacup volume)

FOR EACH CANDLE
1 teacup
1 wick
180g paraffin wax
20g beeswax
½ tbsp stearin (improves the burn)
A few shavings of candle dye or the stub of an old coloured candle (if you want colours)
2 tsp essential oil (if you want scented candles)

<u>*Cleaning:*</u> *Nobody ever mentions this bit when discussing candles, do they? White spirit will melt the wax off your bowl/jug. If you spill some on the table, just wait till it cools and peel it off.*

Clean the teacup well so that it is free of grease and dust. Fill it with water to see how much wax you will need, an average teacup uses about 200ml.

Cut a piece of wick 5cm longer than the height of the cup. Tie it around the middle of a pencil, which you balance on top of the cup. The longer end should hang into the cup. (If you buy cotton core wick from a specialist candle stockist, it is quite stiff, so I just curl it around the pencil to keep the wick central in the cup.) You can also buy a wick sustainer (the little metal disc you find at the bottom of wicks) and hot glue it to the bottom of the teacup, but it is not essential.

Make a bain-marie by heating a couple of cups of boiling water in a medium pan. Place a heatproof bowl on top of the pan so that the bottom of the bowl doesn't touch the water underneath. Put both types of wax and the stearin into the bowl and simmer until the wax melts. Now is the time to add the wax die and the scent, if using.

If your bowl has a pouring lip, pour the wax directly into the teacup. If not, transfer it to an old glass or Pyrex jug before pouring. Make sure the wick is centred.

Leave to cool and harden. If a well forms as it cools, fill it up with more melted wax.

When the candle has cooled, untie the wick from the pencil and cut to size. Leave for a day to settle before burning.

Dressing the Part

Aprons

According to Wikipedia, aprons are 'outer protective garments that cover primarily the front of the body'. Oh no they're not. Aprons confer magical powers, in fact I'd say that aprons 'repel all evil'. I don't know why, but I feel safer wearing an apron. You feel slightly invincible in them.

I have quite the apron collection: big ones, ones with tabards or bibs, linen *Downton Abbey*-style aprons, white French-maid frilly ones, pinafores, retro Doris Day aprons with appliqués and 1950s negligée pinnies in sheer fabrics. In Mexico and Guatemala the women wear aprons all the time, as daywear. Their gingham aprons are gathered at the waist, with lots of zipped pockets, so useful for market trading too. Women wore aprons when clothing was expensive and needed protecting. Nowadays, with cheaper, washable clothing (and washing machines!) it's not such a common garment.

Aprons can be mumsy, in a tongue-in-cheek way, sexy, humorous or practical. The idea of being shielded in an apron isn't just imaginary, it does protect your clothing and, if the apron is thick enough, your skin.

Wonderful aprons can be bought at car boot sales, in French *vide-greniers*, on Etsy, eBay and also at Anthropologie. Don't forget to keep a look out when you are travelling too.

Tea Dresses

Afternoon tea is a rare opportunity to get dressed up. From the 1900s onwards, women entertained at home in 'tea gowns', full-length, Japanese-influenced dresses that wrapped around the body. To make the occasion even more comfortable, one didn't have to wear a corset with a tea gown.

The 1940's 'tea dress' is still worn whenever women wish to feel extra feminine. The tea dress can be worn with heels or flats, buttoned up for a prim look or undone for a more sensual, casual vibe. It suits every figure. The Second World War tea dress often had little puffed sleeves with small pads in the shoulders and a sweetheart neckline. Even during the rationing of the war years women wore florals. In the 1950s 'Horrockses' dresses in bright cotton were the fashion, and in the '60s and '70s, floaty fabrics by Celia Birtwell.

A floral frock is always a lovely choice for afternoon tea. When the garden is blooming and the weather is good, women in Britain dig out the floral frock. You feel feminine, fresh, cheerful, even a little giddy in a flowery dress, with bare legs and open-toed sandals.

The tea dress reflects our mood. The flowery dress can be a language with which the wearer can subtly announce how she is feeling that day. Today I might want to wear bright cartoony dahlias, but for the evening I may don a silky fabric adorned with dark red roses. On other, perhaps quieter, more subdued days, I may choose to dress covered with tiny muted sprigs, Laura Ashley-style. Flowers have symbolic meaning also, according to culture or nationality.

But why stick to flowers? Just as with the garden, I like to mix it up, flowers and vegetables together, so I had my dressmaker, Ruth Bennett, make a tomato dress, an artichoke dress and an aubergine one.

Fascinators, Gloves and Hats

I've had ladies arrive with gorgeous fascinators, a smaller version of a hat, which perches jauntily on the side of the head. I have quite a collection of fascinators. Nobody can ignore you if you wear a hat.

It is a pity that nobody wears gloves these days except Madonna, who wears bizarre leather driving gloves (probably to hide the fact that her hands don't match her face in terms of earth years) and Dot Cotton of *Eastenders*, who is one of the best-dressed women on TV. But gloves are the sort of thing you could absolutely wear to an afternoon tea party. White or pale kid gloves would certainly add to a general atmosphere of elegance and daintiness.

Let's not forget the gentlemen, who can avail themselves of the rare opportunity to wear a waistcoat and bow tie, or cravat and straw hat. They could even go a bit steampunk, with watches on chains, top hats, bowlers and monocles! The formality of an afternoon tea can be an occasion to play dress-up. It's a shame to wear trainers and jeans, don't you think?

I have never passed up on an opportunity to get dressed up!

2. The Savoury Table

The frontal segment of the party is known as savouries and consists of sandwiches, scones and other doughy foods. It is also the time to raid your pantry for curds, jams and pickles.

Sandwiches

A sandwich is a basic building block of after-noon tea and the principal contributor to the savoury part of the meal, so it is important to get it right. Some people – often men – don't ac-tually like too much sweet stuff and are dependent, yes, on a decent selection of sandwiches.

John Montague (1718–1792), 4th Earl of Sandwich, invented the sandwich so that he could continue to eat during card games without getting his paws greasy. A court in Boston declared that a sandwich must include at least two slices of bread, so ideally no pretenders, such as open-faced sandwiches, will be permitted. We aren't allowing triple-deckers either. Afternoon tea isn't American.

Portion-wise, allow 4 to 6 cut sandwiches per person.

When to Make the Sandwiches?

I'd start one to two hours before the event. You don't want a) soggy sandwiches, b) dry, curly sandwiches, c) fridge-cold sandwiches.

What Kind of Bread?

Use light bread or 'Pullman bread', which is bread baked as a rectangle in a long, lidded tin. Afternoon tea is one of the few occasions where it is acceptable, desirable even, to use Chorleywood-processed sliced bread. The Japanese love light airy bread, it's consid-ered a delicacy there. So, unless you are going a bit rustic in style, more *Darling Buds of May* than Duch-ess of Bedford, be guilt-free about buying a moist pre-cut loaf from Warburtons or Kingsmill or whoever. But do buy white and brown bread to alternate.

How to Butter the Bread?

Take a tip from sandwich bars: use a rubber spatula – it's fast and it doesn't tear the bread. Buttering right to the edges prevents sogginess. Use room-temperature butter or cream cheese. Don't use margarine. Marga-rine can be very good in baking but it's absolutely hor-rible in sandwiches. Unless you've got a vegan coming, then of course you can buy suitable soy margarine.

How to Cut the Bread

Use a very sharp knife. Can you sharpen a bread knife? Apparently you can. The scalloped edge is bev-elled on one side only and you need a special 'hon-ing tool'. So, not easy. Therefore only use your bread knife to cut bread, that way it stays in good condition. I often use scissors to remove the crusts. If you are us-ing home-made bread or a crusty loaf, you can buy an electric machine (for about £20) called a bread slicer, which will carve your rustic loaf into thin, neat slices.

Crusts or No Crusts?

No crusts. Unless going rustic (see left). Cut them off after you've made the sandwich, not before. No ends permitted.

Popular Sandwich Shapes

The Rectangle

Cut the bread into thirds. A newspaper article claimed that the Queen and the Royals in general don't like rectangles because it reminds them of coffins. But! Undercover scoop! I heard direct from the mouth of favoured royal jockey Dick Francis's son, who had tea with the Queen Mother several times when she was alive, that she took her sandwiches in rectangles. Who to believe, eh?

The Finger

Cut the bread into quarters, lengthways.

The Triangle

Cut diagonally across the bread into halves or quarters.

The Square

Cut the bread in half, then quarters. Not nearly as popular as the finger or the triangle, but worth knowing about.

The Pinwheel

Trim the crusts from 5 slices of a white or wholemeal sandwich loaf and use a rolling pin to flatten the bread slices slightly. Spread with softened butter or soft spread like cream cheese. Place any toppings along the short end of a slice and from there, start to roll up the slice tightly, without squeezing. Once completely rolled up, wrap each roll tightly in cling film. Refrigerate for 1 hour. Trim the ends using a serrated knife and cut each roll into 6 slices.

The Bum Sandwich

I believe the name of this sandwich was coined by Stefan Gates, an experimental cook and TV broadcaster. His technique is to wrap the sandwich, whichever shape, but a torpedo-shaped sub seems to be a favourite, in cling film, then sit on it, enabling all the flavours to blend under the pressure. Hence the 'bum' sandwich. Possibly this has no place at an elegant tea, but it might be an enjoyable pastime at a children's birthday party.

Savoury Sandwiches

Here are some basic sandwich 'recipes', the classics that anyone might expect to eat at an afternoon tea. You probably have your own favourite combinations, but starting with my trademark ingredient sarnie, here are a few suggestions:

By the way, you butter both slices of bread, not just one.

Marmite Sandwiches

Serves 2

Preferred shape: finger, square or triangle

Butter, at room temperature
Marmite
4 slices white pre-sliced bread
Thin slices of cucumber (optional)
Alfalfa sprouts (optional)
Butter lettuce, washed, dried
  and finely shredded
Freshly ground black pepper, to taste
  (optional)

Now you couldn't have a book written by 'MsMarmitelover' without a Marmite sandwich, could you? It's also the tastiest and simplest savoury, popular with all correct-minded citizens.

You have two possible techniques to use when making a classic Marmite sarnie: you can go the Nigella route, which I like very much, or the more formal route.

1) Nigella method: cream the butter and the marmite together until you have a pleasing caramel colour, to the strength of your choice. Spread it on the bread, edge to edge. Add black pepper to taste, if you like. Close the sandwiches and cut off the crusts. Cut into the shape of your choice.

2) Formal Marmite sarnie recipe: butter the bread, spread on the dose of Marmite (less for children and timorous foreigners), add black pepper to taste, if you like, then close the sandwiches and cut off the crusts. Cut into the shape of your choice.

You can, of course, add cucumber slices, alfalfa sprouts or finely shredded butter lettuce to these marmite sandwiches.

Cheese and Pickle Sandwiches

Serves 2

Preferred shape: triangle

Butter, at room temperature
4 slices white or brown pre-sliced bread
50g Cheddar cheese, either in thin slices
  or grated
4–6 tbsp Branston or home-made pickle,
  or Ikea sweet cucumber pickle (sliced)

Can I ask you to buy another bit of equipment? It's not expensive, honest. Everyone in Scandinavia and the Netherlands has one and it'll totally save your knuckles, because you won't need to grate cheese any more, you'll be slicing. With a cheese slicer. They cost about a fiver. Get one. Everyone who is partial to cheese sandwiches needs one of these in their life. If not for yourself, do it for me, babes.

Butter the bread, edge to edge, then add the cheese, followed by the pickle. Close the sandwiches. Cut off the crusts and cut into a shape. (I think this sandwich suits a triangle. It's like pasta needing a different shape for every sauce. Every sandwich filling suits a different shape.)

Smoked Salmon and Cream Cheese Sandwiches

Serves 3

Preferred shape: square or pinwheel

250g tub of cream cheese
6 slices brown or white pre-sliced bread
250g good-quality smoked salmon,
  thinly sliced
Freshly ground black pepper, to taste
A squeeze of lemon juice

This is the king of sarnies. It's the one that always disappears first from the sandwich platter. Smoked salmon and cream cheese is, famously, also brilliant on bagels, but this is an afternoon tea and we don't do bagels at that time of day, do we? No, we want a slim, soft, salty, pale–pink–and–white sandwich. Fantastic mouthfeel. And it deserves a decent smoked salmon within it. I know it's tempting to buy cheap scraps but, if you can afford to, buy some good stuff (I even smoke my own, as you will see in my previous book *Supper Club*).

Spread the cream cheese on the bread, edge to edge, add a few slices of smoked salmon, grind on some black pepper and squeeze a little lemon juice on to the salmon. Close the sandwiches and trim off the crusts. Cut into the shape of your choice (remembering this also works well as a pinwheel sandwich).

Egg and Cress Sandwiches

Serves 2

Butter, at room temperature
4 slices white or brown pre-sliced bread
40g good-quality mayonnaise
2 tbsp chopped capers
4 hard-boiled eggs, peeled
1 punnet cress or a handful of watercress
Salt and freshly ground black pepper

This is a classic British sandwich, the crisp texture of the cress only serving to underline the comforting flavour of egg, delicate and summery.

Butter the bread, edge to edge. Mix together the mayonnaise and capers, if using, and season to taste with salt and black pepper. Chop the hard-boiled eggs and combine with the mayonnaise mixture. Spread the mixture on to the bread and top with the cress or watercress. Close the sandwiches and cut off the crusts. Cut into the shape of your choice.

Tuna and Mayonnaise Sandwiches

Serves 3

Preferred shape: finger or triangle

Butter, at room temperature
6 slices white or brown pre-sliced bread
135g tin skipjack whole steak tuna in oil
(sunflower or olive), drained and flaked
(but keep the oil)
4 tbsp good-quality mayonnaise (not *low fat*)
Juice of ½ lemon
1 tbsp Dijon or yellow mustard
1 tbsp drained capers or finely sliced
gherkins (optional)
Sea salt and freshly ground black pepper

Tuna and mayonnaise is the sixth most popular sandwich filling in the UK, up thirteen places in recent years, according to a survey by the British Sandwich Association. It's a Jewish deli favourite too, and some people regard it as a blank slate on to which they can add all manner of ingredients, including walnuts, celery, jalapeños, raw onion, lettuce and hummus (?!). I agree with adding a little pickle, but keep it simple, folks. Don't mess with perfection.

Butter the bread, edge to edge. Mix the flaked tuna with the mayonnaise, lemon juice and mustard in a bowl, adding salt and black pepper to taste. Once it's mixed, check for structure, texture and moistness; you may wish to add a little of the drained tuna oil. You may even want to go a little mad and add a few capers or gherkins just to liven it up some more. Spoon it evenly on to half the buttered slices of bread. Close. Trim. Shape.

Cucumber Sandwiches

Serves 2

Preferred shape: finger or square

Butter, at room temperature
4 slices white pre-sliced bread
½ cucumber, peeled and sliced thinly
in rounds
Salt and white pepper

Please note: cucumber sandwiches
are good with Marmite.

According to the chef at the Savoy, we've been making classic cucumber sandwiches wrongly all these years. You aren't supposed to slice the cucumber into circles but, using a peeler, slice it lengthways, very finely, avoiding the seeds. In the interests of research for my readers, I have done a taste test both ways and I'm sorry, Mr Chef at the Savoy, cucumber sandwiches have more crunch if the cucumber is cut into very fine circles. So ignore him and listen to me!

Butter the bread edge to edge, add the cucumber and a light sprinkle of salt and white pepper. Close the sandwiches, trim and shape.

Herb-encrusted Sandwiches

Finely chopped chives or sesame seeds
or poppy seeds

For variety of look and flavour I like to dip the sides of triangular sandwiches into seeds or herbs.

Dip the edges of your chosen sandwich into the chives. Cheese and chives works well, as does cucumber and black sesame seeds.

Jam Sandwiches

Serves 2

Salted butter, at room temperature
4 thick slices of white bloomer
Jam of your choice

This can be done with bloomer
or crusty white bread.

Or a 'bloody bandage' as my great-grandmother called them, when kids used to play in the streets after school, holding a podgy white sandwich in their hands with red jam oozing out. This is less refined but will hit the spot for very hungry or younger guests.

Butter the bread edge to edge, then spread the jam on top. Close the sandwich, and cut in half into a triangle.

Ham and Mustard-pickled Cucumber Sandwiches

Makes 16 mini triangle sandwiches,
with some pickle left over

Preferred shape: triangle

Butter, at room temperature
8 slices white bread, not sourdough
4 slices good-quality country-style ham

FOR THE CUCUMBER PICKLE
1 onion, sliced
2 cucumbers, thinly sliced
1 tbsp pickling salt
1 tsp plain white flour
100g caster sugar
1 tsp yellow mustard seeds
A large pinch of dry mustard powder
A large pinch of celery seeds
A large pinch of ground turmeric
120ml white wine vinegar

This is a guest recipe from Helen Graves, who writes the excellent Food Stories blog. She's such a sandwich fan, she also writes the London review of sandwiches blog and has even written a book on the subject, *101 Sandwiches*. This is her ham sandwich recipe, after all she is an authority on the subject!

For the pickles, put the onion and cucumbers in a colander and sprinkle over the pickling salt. Let the vegetables sit at room temperature (or in the fridge, if you prefer) for at least a few hours, but ideally 8 hours. Rinse and drain, then place in a bowl.

In a small pan, mix together the flour and sugar, then whisk in the mustard seeds and powder, celery seeds, turmeric and vinegar. Bring this mixture to the boil, stirring, and then cook until slightly thickened, about 5–10 minutes. Pour over the vegetables and stir. The pickle is now ready and can be stored in a sealed sterilised jar (see page 41). It is best left for a few days before using.

To make the sandwiches, butter 4 slices of the bread. Lay a slice of ham on each and then add a thin layer of pickle. Top with the other slices of bread and slice each into 4 triangles. Serve.

The Cakewich: the sandwich that looks like a cake!

Serves 20

FOR THE CAKEWICH STRUCTURE
800g cream cheese
1 loaf pre-sliced white bread,
   crusts removed
1 loaf pre-sliced brown bread,
   crusts removed

FOR THE FILLINGS (DEPENDING ON HOW MANY LAYERS YOU HAVE)
1 cucumber, thinly sliced into rounds
500g packet smoked salmon, thinly sliced
2 ripe avocados, halved, stoned and sliced

FOR THE GARNISH
3 cold hard-boiled eggs, peeled
   and thinly sliced
A handful of cress or dill, washed and dried
(You could also add cooked peeled
   prawns, thinly sliced cheese, cold cuts,
   feathery dill sprigs, sliced radishes,
   thinly sliced deseeded red pepper or
   cod's roe. Get creative!)

EQUIPMENT
Star-shaped piping nozzle and a piping
   bag (optional)

Assemble your cakewich on your final serving plate, whether it's a board, large plate, tray or cake stand. You don't want to have to move it later and risk breaking your concoction.

This is not a joke dish. It is something people actually eat in Sweden on special occasions, where it's called a *Smörgåstårta*. It's also a good idea for people who don't eat sugar, as they can have a birthday cake that is savoury! *Smörgåstårta* makes a fantastic centrepiece and is spectacular for kids' parties, too.

This savoury 'rainbow' cake would be a great 'carrier' for leftovers. I've done it with traditional Scandinavian ingredients such as smoked salmon, fish roe, fish roe paste from Kalles and pickled cucumbers. But do use up whatever is in your fridge.

For the cakewich structure, whip the cream cheese in a food processor until it is light and fluffy. Reserve 100g for the crumb coat and 200g for the top coat (spread on the outside of the constructed cakewich, which helps to 'glue' the cakewich together). Spread the white and brown bread slices on both sides with the remaining whipped cream cheese (you do not need to spread the bottom of the bread that will make up your base layer).

Create your base layer with some slices of white bread (cream cheese side up), fitted together tightly. Top with one of the filling ingredients. Do the next layer with brown bread, positioning the slices so that they overlap the white slices underneath, but facing the opposite direction. Top with another of the filling ingredients. Continue to build up your cakewich, alternating between white and brown bread and using a different filling for each layer. Finish with a layer of bread slices on top.

Once the layers are completed, use a rubber spatula to thinly spread the reserved 100g whipped cream cheese around the sides and top of the cakewich to make a crumb coat. Wrap the cakewich and plate/board/stand in cling film, then chill in the fridge for an hour or so to firm up.

Once the cakewich is chilled, spread the remaining 200g whipped cream cheese in an even layer around the cakewich sides and over the top, to create a top coat all over. Garnish the cakewich using any leftover filling ingredients, plus the thinly sliced boiled eggs, the cress and dill. If you like, you could pipe cream cheese rosettes around the edges using a star-shaped piping nozzle. Serve immediately, cut into slices.

A Few Tips:

- *Use a rubber spatula to spread the cream cheese on the bread. Processed bread is soft and difficult to butter when untoasted.*
- *It's easier to make a square or rectangular sandwich cake because of the shape of the bread, but for a more birthday-cake look you could make it round with the aid of a cake tin as a template.*
- *Try to use bread slices of similar dimensions; it makes it easier to assemble, otherwise you will have to do a jigsaw of pieces, although you won't see this once the cakewich is assembled and covered.*
- *You could use mayonnaise instead of cream cheese if you want a lighter cake.*

Sweet Sandwiches

We talk of sandwiches as savoury but, especially abroad,
there is a long tradition of the sweet sandwich.

Sprinkles Sandwiches

Serves 2

Salted butter, at room temperature
4 slices white bread, thinly sliced
Approximately 30g chocolate sprinkles

We call them 'hundreds and thousands', but in the Netherlands the chocolate sprinkles sandwich has become an art form, enjoyed by children and adults alike. The supermarkets stock boxes of different flavoured sprinkles known as *Hagelslag* or 'hailstorm', which you scatter over an open sandwich. The sprinkles come in white, milk or dark chocolate and there are even candy-covered sprinkles in fruit flavours.

Butter the bread edge to edge, then scatter the sprinkles evenly. Close the sandwiches, cut off the crusts and cut into quarters.

Fairy Sandwiches

Serves 2

Salted butter, at room temperature
4 slices white bread, thinly sliced
Approximately 40g of rainbow-coloured
* hundreds and thousands*

This is an Australian delicacy very similar to the *Hagelslag* Dutch sandwiches. Follow the recipe for The Sprinkles Sandwich above but top with 20g rainbow-hued hundreds and thousands instead.

Butter the bread edge to edge, scatter the hundreds and thousands evenly. Close the sandwiches, cut off the crusts and cut into quarters.

Daily Mail Lunchbox Scandal: Smartie Sandwiches

Serves 2

Salted butter, at room temperature
4 slices white bread, thinly sliced
Approximately 40g of Smarties

I cannot resist reading the *Daily Mail* 'sidebar of shame' at least three times a day. This is why the *Daily Mail*, whose politics are in no way adjacent to mine, is the most popular website in the world. Yes, even above the BBC's! One of the stories that caught my eye was the lunchbox scandal of a child in Lincolnshire sent to school with a, wait for it, Smartie Sandwich. Jamie Oliver would not be happy. After tutting at the utter irresponsibility of mothers for a few seconds, I looked at the photo and thought, actually that looks pretty darn delicious. And it was. Fine for a tea party, but probably not for a nutritious school lunch for a growing child.

Butter the bread edge to edge, and scatter or line up the smarties edge to edge. Close the sandwiches, cut off the crusts and cut into halves.

Olive Oil and Chocolate Crostini

Makes approximately 20

1 good-quality French baguette
Extra virgin olive oil, to drizzle
100g good-quality dark chocolate,
  broken into squares
Sea salt, to sprinkle

Crostini and bruschetta are virtually the same thing: toast with something savoury like garlic, olive and tomatoes scraped on top. However, you can make sweet crostini with olive oil. The grassy flavour goes brilliantly with chocolate. In terms of difficulty and time, this recipe couldn't be easier. Make it at the last-minute, just as the guests arrive.

Take the French baguette and cut it into 2.5cm slices at a slight angle. Grill the slices until golden on both sides, then drizzle a little fruity olive oil over one side of each slice. Top each one with a square or two of dark chocolate and return them to the grill for a few seconds to melt the chocolate. Sprinkle a little sea salt on top, and serve.

Savoury Spreads

Mackerel Pâté

Makes 1 small jar

2 hot-smoked mackerel fillets, skinned
Juice of 1 lemon
1 tbsp freshly grated (peeled) horseradish,
    or failing that, creamy horseradish sauce
100ml crème fraîche
A handful of chopped fresh parsley
A handful of snipped fresh chives
Freshly ground black pepper, to taste

An intense and savoury sandwich filling.

Put everything into a food processor and whizz together until smooth. This spread will last for up to 2 days in the fridge. It's a bracing savoury to use on toast or in sandwiches. If you want a more Scandinavian flavour, use fresh dill instead of parsley. By the way, I always keep a stick of fresh horseradish in my freezer (along with fresh root ginger), so that I can grate it whenever I need it.

Coren's Patum Peperium

Makes 1 small jar

1 tbsp capers, drained
1 fresh red chilli, deseeded
5–6 tinned anchovies in oil, drained
100g salted butter, at room temperature
Freshly ground black pepper, to taste

I've just realised I've been pronouncing this wrongly for years, as Patum Peporium, probably because it's quite peppery. It's the sort of thing you know your dad will like. It's so hard to buy presents for men, so I used to buy my dad tubs of this for Christmas. One tiny and intense china pot would last for a year.

So, I was looking around for how to make it and I realised there was a very simple recipe on one of my favourite food blogs, Recipe Rifle, by Esther Coren. Her blog, about raising young children and learning to cook, is both truthful and funny. 'Can I use it?' I asked Esther on Twitter. 'It's actually by Giles, but yes, he will be delighted,' she replied. Her husband is Giles Coren, the restaurant critic of the *Sunday Times*, so he knows his stuff when it comes to food.

Chop up the capers, chilli and anchovies together and then, using the side of a knife or a spatula, mash the butter into the spicy mix with a few grinds of black pepper. It's easiest then to sling all the ingredients into a food processor, but if you don't have one, use a pestle and mortar to bash them into a smooth paste. Scrape into a ceramic ramekin and cover. This will last for up to 10 days in the fridge. Meltingly delicious on toast and in sandwiches.

Sandwich Spread

Makes 1 small jar

100ml Heinz salad cream
1 carrot, finely diced
¼ stick celery, finely diced
5–6 gherkins, drained and finely diced
½ red pepper, deseeded and finely diced
1 tsp Dijon mustard or any mild
   non-grainy mustard
Sea salt, to taste

Remember this? Remember salad cream, before we discovered proper mayonnaise? My nan always had 'sandwich spread' on the tea table. For those who love nostalgia, here is a home-made version.

Mix all the ingredients together, then chill and use in sandwiches.

Pantry Goods
Curds, Jams & Creams

For each of these recipes for curd or jam, sterilise two standard (450g) jam jars by putting them through the dishwasher on a hot wash or rinsing them in hot water, then placing them in a preheated oven at 180°C (gas 4) for 15 minutes. (I stand them, open side up, spaced so they aren't touching, on a baking sheet lined with a tea towel or newspaper). Use new lids each time you make jam. If you haven't got new lids, then have cellophane discs ready for the tops of the jars (as well as the wax discs).

These curds are great piped into doughnuts or used for pies or on toast for breakfast or afternoon tea. They last a couple of weeks in the fridge, so use them quickly.

Passion Fruit Curd

Makes enough for 2 standard
(450g) jam jars

4–5 passion fruits, halved and flesh
  scooped out
175g caster sugar
100g cold unsalted butter, cubed
2 large eggs, plus 1 large egg yolk, beaten
A pinch of sea salt

Yolk-yellow, tangy-sweet curd with a twist. Use on scones, on toast, on teacakes, in tarts, to sandwich sponge cakes, in yoghurt... Eat it quickly, it doesn't last long. Passion fruit are ripe when the fruit are crinkly, not smooth.

Put the passion fruit flesh, sugar and butter into a pan over a low heat and cook slowly, stirring constantly, to form a smooth custard. It should reach about 70°C and take about 10 minutes.

Remove from the heat and gradually stir in the beaten eggs and egg yolk. Add the salt. Strain the seeds from the curd and pour into the sterilised jam jars, cover and seal, then leave to cool before refrigerating. Keep in the fridge and use within 2 weeks.

Sweet/Sour Gooseberry Curd and Why I Love Twitter!

Makes enough for 2 standard
(450g) jam jars

450g gooseberries, topped and tailed
175g caster sugar
100g cold unsalted butter, cubed
2 large eggs, plus 1 large egg yolk
A pinch of sea salt

After I had complained on Twitter about the price of gooseberries, a lovely lady from Norfolk chimed in, saying she had tons of them in her garden. She met me at King's Cross station in London, platform $9\frac{3}{4}$, near where Boudicca is reputed to be buried, to do a secret handover of a large bag of gooseberries. I couldn't have been more thrilled. So that weekend, armed with my bounty, I went mad on gooseberry recipes: my favourite was this sweet/sour curd.

In my parents' old house in Highgate, north London, there was a gooseberry bush at the bottom of the garden and as a child I was disappointed by the sour taste of the bright green fruit. Back then, gooseberry was another name for the devil, and eating them was the punishment for losing games. Today, sour flavours such as pomegranate, hibiscus, lemon and lime are among my favourites.

This mixture can be spooned into tartlets, spread on toast or scones or, yes, piped into doughnuts.

Rinse the gooseberries, put them into a pan, add enough water to just cover the fruit and cook over a low heat until the gooseberries have burst and become soft. Remove from the heat, then press the gooseberry mixture through a chinois or sieve into another pan, pushing it through with a wooden spoon or spatula.

Add the sugar and butter to the gooseberry mixture while it's still hot, stirring until they are incorporated. Working quickly, whisk the eggs and egg yolk and add them into the mix, along with the salt.

Put the pan back over a low heat and stir continuously until the mixture is thick and custard-like (taking care not to let the mixture boil, otherwise it will curdle). This can take about 20 minutes.

Take the curd off the heat and pour into your sterilised jam jars (see page 41), cover and seal, then leave to cool before refrigerating. Put on a pretty label and keep in the fridge for up to 2 weeks.

Strawberry, Champagne and Vanilla Jam

Makes enough for 2 standard
(450g) jam jars

1kg strawberries, hulled
1kg jam sugar (if you can't get hold of jam
sugar, use ordinary sugar, but the jam
will be runnier)
Juice of ½ lemon
1 bottle (75cl) champagne, cava or prosecco
1 vanilla pod

EQUIPMENT
3 saucers, chilled in the freezer
Wax disks
Jam funnel (buy this, it's very cheap and can
be used generally for pouring into jars)

Pop the saucers in the freezer the night before
so that they're ready for testing the jam.

I'm lucky enough to have tiny wild strawberries in my garden that naturally have an almost vanilla flavour. This recipe tries to recreate an entire cream tea in a jar.

You don't have to use real champagne: cava or prosecco work too. Jams are obviously important for scones but this can also be used for the Giant Custard Cream Jammie Dodger (page 87) or a classic Victoria sponge. If you are going to get into jam making, buy a preserving pan. The traditional copper ones (copper conducts heat very well) can sometimes be bought very cheaply at car boot sales in France. I'm always on the look out.

Scatter the strawberries with half of the sugar the night before you plan to make your jam and leave them to macerate at room temperature overnight.

The next day, place the strawberries into a large pan (preferably a proper preserving pan) over a low heat. Add the rest of the sugar, the lemon juice, champagne and vanilla pod. If the lemon is unwaxed, toss it into the mix, it adds to the pectin. Once the sugar is dissolved, bring the mixture to a rolling boil, then boil hard for about 5 minutes.

To test the setting point, take a saucer from the freezer, and move the jam off the heat. Use a wooden spoon to drop some jam on to the saucer. If you can then push the jam on the saucer with your finger and it wrinkles, it has reached setting point. If not, return the jam to the heat and continue boiling hard. Test the setting point every 10 minutes or so, returning the pan to the heat and the saucer to the freezer each time, until the jam has reached setting point. It takes on average about 30 minutes to reach setting point. This is one technique. If you have a sugar thermometer, the jam is set once it reaches 104.5°C. Experienced jam-makers also notice that the bubbles in the jam are smaller and tighter as it approaches setting point.

Once the jam has reached setting point, take the pan off the heat and let the jam settle for a few minutes, remove and discard the vanilla pod and lemon half, then pour the jam into the sterilised jars (see page 41) using a jam funnel if you have one. Press down a wax disc to form a seal on top of the jam. Screw on the lids. Make pretty labels and mark them with the date and flavour of your jam. Unopened, this will last for up to a year, but once opened, store in the fridge.

Home–made Organic Sweetened Condensed Milk

Makes 250ml

1 litre organic whole milk
450g organic granulated sugar

If you are boycotting Nestlé, you can make your own organic condensed milk. It isn't quite as sweet as the tinned stuff, either.

Put the milk and sugar into a heavy-based pan over a medium-high heat. Bring to the boil, then turn down the heat to very low and simmer, uncovered, for 2 hours, stirring regularly with a spatula. You'll need to stir it more frequently towards the end, and if it does become lumpy, just whizz it until smooth using a hand-held stick blender.

Remove the pan from the heat, cover with a tea towel and leave to cool. Pour into a sterilised container (see page 41), cover and seal, then refrigerate. It will keep in the fridge for up to 2 weeks.

Rose Butter

Makes 100g

100g good-quality unsalted butter
Rose petals

This is a perfumed and pretty butter for delicate finger sandwiches. Line the bottom of a jar with a thick layer of fresh rose petals. Wrap 100g good-quality unsalted butter with waxed paper, and place it in the jar. Cover with more rose petals. Cover the jar and leave it to sit in a cool place overnight. If you want to incorporate any of the rose petals into the butter, cut out the bitter yellow 'heel' of the petals with a pair of scissors and finely chop the petals.

Clotted Cream

Makes 250g

400ml thick double cream

Warm the double cream in a bain-marie (see page 69), making sure the bowl doesn't touch the simmering water underneath. Heat gently, without stirring, until the cream is reduced by half and has a texture like butter with a crust. Do not let the cream boil. Take the 'butter' off the heat and leave it to cool. Cover the top of the bowl with cling film and leave it in the fridge for a couple of hours. Skim off the thick crust. This is your clotted cream.

Home-made 'Nutella'

Makes 2 x 200g jars

200g whole hazelnuts, shelled
350g milk chocolate, chopped
2 tbsp groundnut or hazelnut oil
3 tbsp icing sugar
1 tbsp unsweetened cocoa powder
½ tsp vanilla extract
¾ tsp sea salt or vanilla salt

The thing I don't like about Nutella is the claggy palm oil sensation in your mouth. The home-made version means you know exactly what's going into it.

First, toast the hazelnuts. Preheat the oven to 180°C (gas 4). Place the hazelnuts in a single layer on a baking sheet and toast them in the oven for 5–10 minutes, watching that they don't burn. Remove from the oven and carefully rub off the papery skins using a rough tea towel. Leave to cool.

Melt the chocolate in a bain-marie (a heatproof bowl set over a pan of gently simmering water), making sure the bowl doesn't touch the simmering water underneath, or melt it in a bowl in short bursts in the microwave (on full power). (If you have a strong blender you don't need to melt the chocolate, just grind all the ingredients together.)

Grind the toasted hazelnuts with the remaining ingredients in a blender until they form a paste, adding the melted milk chocolate. The paste will thicken as it cools. It keeps for up to 1 month in an airtight container in the fridge. Use in sandwiches or on toast.

Scones, Teacakes, Muffins and more

Curds and jams are the perfect accompaniments to scones and bannocks, which usually follow the sandwiches in a traditional afternoon tea and make a nice bridge between the savoury and sweet courses.

Scones

Makes 6–8

250g plain flour, plus extra for dusting
1 tsp cream of tartar
1 tsp bicarbonate of soda
1 heaped tbsp caster sugar
1 tsp custard powder
½ tsp sea salt
55g cold unsalted butter, cubed
150ml buttermilk
1 egg, beaten, to glaze

Variation: For the Oriental-themed Afternoon Tea (see page 206), you could make Matcha Scones. Just add 1–2 teaspoons matcha (a finely ground green tea powder) to the dry mix.

Scones are the source of much dispute: from how to pronounce the word – 'scon', 'scohne' or even 'skoon' – to whether you put the clotted cream or the jam on first. In Cornwall, the jam goes first; in Devon, the cream. Ergonomically, it makes sense to put the jam first, but visually I go with Devon's thick knot of clotted cream punctuated sharply with a dollop of crimson jam!

However you pronounce the word and whichever way you eat them, scones are another essential constituent of British afternoon tea.

Preheat the oven to 180°C (gas 4). Line a baking sheet with parchment paper or a silicone mat.

Sift the flour into a bowl and mix in the cream of tartar, bicarbonate of soda, sugar, custard powder and salt. Add the butter and rub it in with your fingertips until the mixture resembles fine breadcrumbs.

Make a well in the centre and pour in the buttermilk. Use a fork to work it into the dry ingredients. Finish by kneading the mixture lightly (chaffing) by hand on a lightly floured work surface until it forms a soft dough. Pat or roll out the dough into a solid shape about 3cm thick.

Dip a plain round cutter or the top of a glass (about 5–6cm in diameter) into flour, then cut the dough into rounds. Don't twist the cutter or glass or your scones will bake wonky. Place them on the prepared baking sheet.

Glaze the tops with the beaten egg and bake for 15–20 minutes, until risen and golden. Transfer to a wire rack and leave to cool. Serve warm or cold, split and topped with butter, jam and clotted cream.

Blueberry Scones

Makes about 12

450g self-raising flour, plus extra for dusting
75g caster sugar
1 tbsp custard powder
1 tsp sea salt
175g cold unsalted butter, cubed
2 large eggs, beaten, plus extra for glazing
90ml buttermilk
1 punnet fresh blueberries (about 100–150g)

I confess, I can find scones a little boring. Adding fruit such as blueberries both moistens the fudgy texture and brightens it with bursts of flavour.

Preheat the oven to 180°C (gas 4). Line a baking sheet with parchment paper or a silicone mat.

Mix the dry ingredients together in a bowl, then add the butter and rub it in with your fingertips until the mixture resembles fine breadcrumbs. Make a well in the centre and pour in the eggs and buttermilk. Work the wet ingredients into the dry ingredients. It will look quite wet, but do not be tempted to add more flour. Mix in the blueberries.

'Chaff' the dough by kneading it lightly 2 or 3 times on a lightly floured work surface, until it forms a soft dough. Pat or roll out the dough into a solid shape about 3cm thick.

Dip a plain round cutter or the top of a glass (about 5–6cm in diameter) into flour, then cut the dough into rounds. Don't twist the cutter or glass or your scones will not be straight. Place them on the prepared baking sheet.

Glaze the tops with extra beaten egg and bake for 15–20 minutes, until risen and golden. Transfer to a wire rack and leave to cool. Serve warm or cold, split and spread with jam and clotted cream.

Bannocks

Makes 12

450g plain flour, plus extra for dusting
½ tsp baking powder
1 tsp sea salt
300–350ml buttermilk

EQUIPMENT
Heavy-based griddle or frying pan

Bannocks are scones from the Shetlands, islands so far north of Scotland that they are closer to the Arctic Circle than to Britain. Shetland was for centuries part of Norway and Denmark (which used to be one kingdom), and became Scottish only in the 15th century. In fact, Denmark still has rights to Shetland, having merely pawned the islands. (Shetland is traditionally Unionist, preferring to be part of the UK rather than be independent. This could be a concern for a separatist Scotland, as the Shetland islands are where most of the oil is found.)

Visiting Shetland in June meant that I got to experience the eerie 'simmer dim', the sun shining at midnight. I got this recipe from a remarkable old cookery book called *Recipes for Northern Wives* by Miss Margaret B. Stout, a record of the hardy but simple recipes of Shetland women using local produce.

I made two types: 'top' bannocks, as a lady I met in the supermarket called them, cooked on a griddle (probably even better on a peat fire); and, presumably, 'bottom' bannocks, baked in the oven. Roll them out a bit thinner if you are cooking them on the griddle or in a dry frying pan, otherwise they can remain uncooked in the middle.

Eat, spread generously with butter, perhaps with a boiled kipper or some Mackerel Pâté (see page 39), and serve with a glass of cold buttermilk.

Mix the dry ingredients together in a bowl, then make into a soft dough with the buttermilk, just as soft as can be easily handled. Turn the dough out on to a floured board and form into 12 patties, each about 6–7cm diameter and 8mm thick. I like them to look quite rough and not too smooth.

Cook them either on a dry griddle or in a dry frying pan, over a low heat, for about 10 minutes, until risen and golden on the outside, turning once. Alternatively, place them on a baking sheet and bake in a preheated oven at 180°C (gas 4) for about 15 minutes. Transfer to a wire rack to cool.

Teacakes

Makes 8

500g strong white bread flour, plus extra
    for dusting
2 tbsp caster sugar
1 tbsp ground cinnamon
1 tbsp ground mixed spice
1 tsp ground nutmeg
Finely grated zest of ½ orange
1 tsp sea salt
1 sachet (7g) fast-action dried yeast
330ml milk
A few drops of rose water or orange-
    blossom water (optional)
130g sultanas (you can hydrate/soak them
    in a little sherry beforehand, if you wish)
Melted butter, for glazing

Or currant cakes as they call them in the north of England, where
they are commonly split in half, toasted, buttered and eaten with
Marmite. You could add a few drops of rose water to the dough
for a Tudor 'manchet' feel.

Line a baking sheet with parchment paper or a silicone mat.

Mix the flour, sugar, spices, orange zest, salt and yeast together
in a bowl. Warm the milk slightly (not too hot or you will kill the
yeast) and add it to the flour mixture, along with the rose water
or orange-blossom water, if using. Knead to combine and make a
dough, then add the sultanas. They may pop out but keep kneading
for about 10 minutes or so. Leave the dough in a covered bowl in a
warm place for an hour or so, until it has doubled in size.

Carefully scrape the dough on to a lightly floured surface and cut
it into 8 equal pieces, around 125g each. Tuck each piece into a flattened ball shape with the seam underneath, and lay them on the prepared baking sheet. Cover and leave in a warm place for 30 minutes.

Preheat the oven to 180°C (gas 4).

Glaze the teacakes with the melted butter and bake for 20 minutes, until risen and golden. Transfer to a wire rack to cool. Eat
warm with butter or serve toasted with butter. These teacakes freeze
well for up to 1 month.

Cornish Splits from Miss Foodwise

Makes about 24

14g dried yeast
2 tsp caster sugar
355ml milk, lukewarm
115g good-quality unsalted butter
30g solid vegetable fat, such as Trex or lard
750g strong white bread flour
1 heaped tsp sea salt
Melted unsalted butter, for brushing the
    buns (optional)

Regula Ysewijn is a Belgian food blogger (her blog is Miss Food-wise), graphic designer and photographer, who is in love with British food culture. Her dream is to end up in the English countryside rearing pigs!

These buns are a traditional regional alternative to the classic scone. A classic way of preparing them is called 'Thunder and Lightning': split the freshly baked buns in half and fill with golden syrup or black treacle and Cornish clotted cream.

In a small bowl, mix the yeast and sugar in a couple of tablespoons of the lukewarm milk and leave for about 10 minutes or so to allow the yeast to activate (a frothy head will develop on top).

Heat the butter and vegetable shortening or lard in a small pan over a low heat. In a large bowl, combine the melted fats with the flour, salt and half of the remaining milk. Add the yeast mixture and combine. Add the rest of the milk and knead for 10 minutes.

Place the dough back in the bowl, cover with a clean tea towel and leave it to rise in a warm place for 45–60 minutes or until the dough has doubled in size.

Line a baking sheet with parchment paper or grease the baking sheet with melted butter.

Tip the dough out on to a work surface, knock it back, knead it again and then shape into a long sausage. Divide the dough into equal-sized pieces of 40–50g each and roll them into balls. Place your buns, evenly spaced, on the prepared baking sheet. Cover and leave to rise in a warm place for 30 minutes, until doubled in size.

Preheat the oven to 220°C (gas 7).

Bake the buns for 20 minutes or until risen and golden. Classic food writer Florence White recommends that when you remove them from the oven, you rub or brush the buns all over with some melted butter and wrap them in a clean tea towel to cool, so that they don't develop a crust.

You can keep these little buns for 4 days in an airtight container. Before use, reheat them in a hot oven (with a small container of water placed at the bottom of the oven to add steam) for about 6 minutes.

Enjoy with clotted cream and jam, or with clotted cream and golden syrup or black treacle.

Crumpets

Makes 12

70g strong white bread flour
70g plain white flour
1 sachet (7g) fast-action dried yeast
½ tsp sea salt
1 tsp caster sugar
275ml milk, warm (not hot)
¼ tsp bicarbonate of soda
75–100ml warm water
Melted unsalted butter, for greasing
Lots of salty butter, for spreading!

EQUIPMENT
Cast-iron or good-quality heavy-based
    frying pan (or griddle)
At least 4 metal crumpet or egg rings or
    plain metal pastry cutters about 7.5cm
    in diameter
Heatproof pastry brush

How to achieve holes:
• Beat the batter sufficiently.
• Don't overfill the rings with batter.
• Cook the crumpets very slowly so that
    the bubbles have enough time to form
    and then pop.

Lots of people are making crumpets these days, but the real trick is to get enough holes into them. Flat crumpets have nowhere for the butter to sink into! I love crumpets with Marmite, but you could also reserve a little of the batter to make flavoured crumpets with orange-blossom water and spread them with honey. You can go free-form or use greased crumpet or egg rings to get the perfect shape.

If you want a slightly sourdough flavour in your crumpets, make the batter the night before, but don't add the bicarb yet. Leave the batter covered overnight at room temperature and add the bicarb in the morning, then cook the crumpets for breakfast. This slow fermentation will also aid in the ongoing quest for holes in your crumpets.

Mix together the flours, yeast and salt. Add the sugar and milk and beat until you have a smooth batter. Cover and leave to rise for 45 minutes.

Combine the bicarbonate of soda with the warm water and mix it into the batter. Cover again and rest for 20 minutes.

Prepare your pan by heating it up. I keep a little pot of the butter, a pastry brush and the batter with a small ladle next to the hob.

Butter the pan and sufficiently grease the insides of the rings or cutters, using the pastry brush. Allow the rings to heat up in the pan, then, using a tablespoon or a small ladle, fill each ring to a depth of about 2cm. You don't want to overfill as your crumpets will take too long to cook and the holes won't have enough time to form.

Wait. Be patient. Turn your crumpets over only once you can see holes starting to poke through the batter. Then, using tongs or the corner of a tea towel, lift away the rings and flip over the crumpets to continue cooking.

Brush the empty rings with more butter and ladle in more batter.

To keep the crumpets hot, lay them one by one in a large 'envelope' of tin foil and keep them in the oven on its lowest heat. Even better, butter them copiously and rush them out to your guests, piping hot!

English Muffins

Makes 10

300g strong white bread flour, plus extra
    for dusting
1 tsp sea salt
½ tsp caster sugar
2 tsp fast-action dried yeast
250ml milk, lukewarm
1 tbsp melted unsalted butter, plus extra
    for greasing
Fine cornmeal or semolina, for dusting

EQUIPMENT
7cm round biscuit cutter
Heavy-based frying pan or griddle

English muffins were one of the earliest foods to be eaten with afternoon tea, served on silver muffin dishes and particularly popular in the 18th century. Muffin dishes, now found only in antique shops, were used to serve breads, pastries and muffins. They consisted of three parts: a base into which fitted a tray, and then a domed lid. Hot water was poured into the base, the muffins were added to the tray, and the lid kept them warm throughout tea time.

Nowadays, it appears to be our ex-colonial cousins in America who have kept English muffins going as a culinary concern, but for breakfast rather than tea. English muffins are not to be confused with those mountainous cupcake-style muffins they sell in coffee shops.

Sift the flour, salt and sugar into a large bowl and stir in the yeast. Make a well in the centre and add the warm milk and melted butter. Mix well to form a sticky dough.

Turn the dough out on to a well-floured surface. Knead until it loses its stickiness, sifting more flour on to the surface as required. Once the dough has lost its stickiness, continue to knead for 10 minutes. The dough should be soft and elastic.

Put the dough into a lightly greased bowl, cover and leave in a warm place for about 1 hour or until the dough has doubled in size. Turn the dough out on to a floured surface, knock it back and then roll it out to about 1cm thick.

Use the biscuit cutter to cut out rounds. Sprinkle some cornmeal or semolina on to a flat surface and place the muffins on top. Sprinkle the tops with cornmeal or semolina. Cover and leave to prove (rise) in a warm place for about 45 minutes.

Place a lightly greased frying pan or griddle over a medium-low heat. Add the muffins (in batches) to the pan. Cook gently on one side for 5 minutes, then turn and cook on the other side for 4–5 minutes. Turn one last time and cook for 2–3 minutes, until cooked and golden all over. Transfer to a wire rack and leave to cool.

Serve warm or toasted, split and spread lavishly with butter. A trick for splitting them is to go around the middle with a fork rather than a knife, to get that authentic American English muffin look.

Rachel's Secret Tea Room Muffins

Makes 12

250g self-raising flour
1 tsp bicarbonate of soda
85g salted butter, melted
2 large eggs, beaten
284ml buttermilk
A handful of chopped fresh herbs,
   including chives, thyme and basil
100g Hazelwood cheese or fresh Parmesan
   cheese, grated

EQUIPMENT
12-hole muffin tray
12 paper muffin cases

These are the other type of muffin, which are more like savoury cupcakes (see picture overleaf).

Rachel runs a secret tea room in her living room in Belper, Derbyshire (see page 248), and has always been a baking fanatic. She works in local government, but went part-time to give herself more time to spend on her passion! 'When I have a mixed party of guests who do not know one another and I hear the chatter and laughter, it makes it so worthwhile,' she says.

'My recipe is for Hazelwood Cheese and Herb Muffins. Hazelwood cheese is locally made in Hazelwood, which is just down the road from where I live. It has quite a strong flavour but is fantastic in these muffins, very more-ish. The plate is quickly cleared when they appear at the table slightly warm.'

Preheat the oven to 200°C (gas 6). Line the muffin tray with paper muffin cases.

In a bowl, combine the flour and bicarbonate of soda. In a jug, mix together the melted butter, eggs and buttermilk. Combine the wet and dry ingredients in the bowl, but do not over-mix. Add the chopped herbs and most of the cheese, reserving a little to sprinkle over the muffins.

Spoon the muffin mix evenly into the cases and sprinkle with the remaining cheese. Bake for 15–18 minutes, until golden brown and firm. Transfer to a wire rack to cool. Serve slightly warm.

Little Teacup Soups

Watercress Soup

Serves 4–6

2 shallots, finely chopped
50g unsalted butter
1 heaped tbsp plain flour
250g watercress (reserve a few leaves for
 the garnish)
400ml milk
100ml double cream (reserve a little to serve)
Sea salt and freshly ground black pepper

As well as forming a highly traditional and refreshing English summertime soup, watercress is reputed to be anti-ageing, reducing wrinkles and combatting free radicals. (Who are the free radicals? Why is their main policy to make people look older?) Personally I think the main ingredient to looking good over 40 is to have lots of money, plenty of holidays and to drink olive oil by the gallon. But if watercress soup will help, who am I to argue? Serve this in teacups, either chilled or warmed up.

Fry the shallots in the butter in a pan until soft. Add the flour and stir to combine, then add the watercress and stir for a couple of minutes. Finally, add the milk and cream. Warm through for 2–3 minutes, then either blend with a hand-held stick blender or pour the soup into a food processor and blend at high speed until smooth. Season to taste with salt and black pepper.

Serve chilled or warmed up in teacups, with a swirl of cream and a few watercress leaves to garnish.

Strawberry and Hibiscus Soup

Serves 4–6

50g dried hibiscus flowers
500ml hot water
450g ripe strawberries, hulled (reserve a
 few for the decoration)
100g caster sugar
5cm piece fresh root ginger, peeled and
 roughly chopped
2 tbsp pomegranate syrup

Hibiscus, known as *Jamaica* in Mexico, is full of vitamin C and is also known to deter diabetes and balance blood-sugar levels. Drinking 3 cups a day can lower your blood pressure by 13 per cent, a recent study showed. Hibiscus denotes the exotic dried red flowers rather than the leaves, known as sorrel. It works well as a cold drink, mixed with agave syrup, and for hot teas. Hibiscus matches beautifully with strawberries to make this refreshing dessert soup, which can be served in teacups or pretty soup bowls.

Soak the hibiscus flowers in the hot water in a bowl and leave to stand for a couple of hours or overnight, then strain the flavoured water into a jug.

Place the strawberries in a blender and pour in the hibiscus water, then add the sugar, ginger and pomegranate syrup. Blend on high until smooth and well mixed.

Serve in teacups, garnished with the reserved strawberries.

Savoury Tartlets

For a little variety, serve some warm tartlets alongside your sandwiches and scones. If you keep them small, then everyone gets their own little treat.

Blue Cheese Tartlets

Makes 4–8 tartlets
(depending on the size of your tins)

150g plain flour
A pinch of sea salt
50ml olive oil, plus extra for oiling the
    work surface
200ml water
200g blue cheese, crumbled (you can use
    any blue cheese you have to hand)
4 eggs
300ml crème fraîche
Melted butter, for greasing

EQUIPMENT
4–8 x 5–10cm loose-based tartlet tins
    (depending on how many you possess,
    you may have to cook these tartlets in
    batches)

I first came up with this recipe while staying in a chalet in the French Alps. The saltiness of the blue cheese is nicely set off by the crème fraîche.

Preheat the oven to 180°C (gas 4). Grease the tartlet tins with melted butter.

In a bowl, mix together the flour and salt, then add the olive oil and water. Work the pastry until it comes together, adding a little more water if necessary.

Roll out the pastry on an oiled work surface until it is 2–3mm thick. Using the bottom of your tartlet tins as a guide, cut out the pastry into rounds slightly bigger than the diameter of the tins. Place a round of pastry into each tin, pressing it evenly over the base and up the sides of the tin. (If pieces break off or you cannot roll it out big enough, just press the pieces back into the tartlet tins.) This is a deliciously crumbly pastry. These pastry cases don't require blind-baking, but prick the bottom of each tartlet case with a fork. Brush the rims of the pastry cases with melted butter or olive oil.

In another bowl, whisk together the blue cheese, eggs and crème fraîche and then pour the mixture into the pastry cases.

Bake for 40 minutes or until the pastry begins to turn golden. Transfer to a wire rack to cool. Carefully remove the tartlets from the tins to serve and serve warm or cold.

Tomato and Anchovy Tartlets

Makes 4–8 tartlets
(depending on the size of your tins)

150g plain flour
A pinch of sea salt
50ml olive oil, plus extra for oiling the
    work surface
200ml water
Melted butter, for greasing

CHOICE OF FILLINGS
Tomato purée
A smear of pesto, red or green
Cherry tomatoes, halved
Tinned anchovies in oil, drained
Pitted black olives (left whole, halved or
    sliced – the choice is yours)
Caperberries, drained
Marinated artichoke hearts, drained and
    quartered

Rosemary salt (a mix of dried rosemary
and sea salt), for sprinkling

EQUIPMENT
4–8 x 5–10cm loose-based tartlet tins
    (depending on how many you possess,
    you may have to cook these tartlets in
    batches)

This recipe is intensely flavoursome, a delicious savoury small tartlet 'pizzete' before you get stuck into the sweet cake. You can play around with fillings, arranging the anchovies, olives, capers and tomatoes into different designs. The ingredients are Italian–influenced; think of them as mini antipasti with a pastry base.

Preheat the oven to 180°C (gas 4). Grease the tartlet tins with melted butter.

In a bowl, mix together the flour and salt, then add the olive oil and water. Work the pastry until it comes together, adding a little more water if necessary.

Roll out the pastry on an oiled work surface until it is 2–3mm thick. Using the bottom of your tartlet tins as a guide, cut out the pastry into rounds slightly bigger than the diameter of the tins. Place a round of pastry into each tin, pressing it evenly over the base and up the sides of the tin. (If pieces break off or you cannot roll it out big enough, just press the pieces back into the tartlet tins.) This is a deliciously crumbly pastry. These pastry cases don't require blind-baking, but prick the bottom of each tartlet case with a fork. Brush the rims of the pastry cases with melted butter or olive oil.

Carefully fill the pastry cases with a combination of the fillings, arranging the ingredients prettily, making sure the tomato purée and pesto are at the bottom.

Bake for about 30 minutes or until the tomato halves (if using) are roasted and the pastry begins to turn golden. Transfer to a wire rack to cool. Carefully remove the tartlets from the tins to serve. Sprinkle with a little rosemary salt and serve warm or cold.

Spirally Veggie Tartlets

Makes 4–8 tartlets
(depending on the size of your tins)

150g plain flour
A pinch of sea salt
50ml olive oil, plus extra for
    oiling the work surface
200ml water
200ml milk
2 eggs
2 sprigs of fresh lemon thyme,
    leaves picked
2 carrots, ends trimmed
2 courgettes, ends trimmed
2–4 feta-stuffed green olives, halved
    (optional)
Melted butter, for greasing
Sea salt and freshly ground black pepper

EQUIPMENT
4–8 x 5–10cm loose-based tartlet tins
    (depending on how many you possess, you
    may have to cook these tartlets in batches)

These delicate vegetable tartlets will delight both the palate and the eye. They are a little bit fiddly to make but worth the effort.

Preheat the oven to 180°C (gas 4). Grease the tartlet tins with melted butter.

In a bowl, mix together the flour and salt, then add the olive oil and water. Work the pastry until it comes together, adding a little more water if necessary.

Roll out the pastry on an oiled work surface until it is 2–3mm thick. Using the bottom of your tartlet tins as a guide, cut out the pastry into rounds slightly bigger than the diameter of the tins. Place a round of pastry into each tin, pressing it evenly over the base and up the sides of the tin. (If pieces break off or you cannot roll it out big enough, just press the pieces back into the tartlet tins.) This is a deliciously crumbly pastry. These pastry cases don't require blind-baking, but prick the bottom of each tartlet case with a fork. Brush the rims of the pastry cases with melted butter or olive oil.

In another bowl, whisk together the milk and eggs, add the thyme and season with salt and black pepper.

Use a vegetable peeler to finely slice the carrots and courgettes lengthways into thin ribbons like wide tagliatelle. Depending on the depth of your tartlet tins, you may need to cut the ribbons in half lengthways.

Curl the vegetable ribbons into the pastry cases in spirals, alternating between carrot and courgette ribbons. The circles will get smaller as you get towards the centre. Place half a stuffed olive in the centre of each tartlet, if you like. Carefully pour the milk and egg mixture into the pastry cases and season with a little more black pepper.

Bake for 40 minutes or until the pastry begins to turn golden. Transfer to a wire rack to cool. Carefully remove the tartlets from the tins to serve and serve warm or cold.

3. The Sweet Table

Although I've put an emphasis on having enough savouries at an afternoon tea, what people really expect is sugary food, especially cake. Afternoon tea is fundamentally a sweet meal with liquid refreshment. You are not simply allowed to eat lots of cake, it is virtually required. How great is that? After all, an afternoon tea party is a rare treat, a special occasion, not something we have every day.

Equipment for Baking

Baking sheet (a very flat one) for biscuit-making (a couple or so are handy to have).

Balloon whisk or electric hand-held whisk.

Big electric stand mixer from Kitchenaid or Kenwood (if you can afford it). It's a big investment, I know, but it makes life so much easier, and it'll last forever.

Biscuit/cookie cutters.

Cake tins/moulds in different sizes and shapes, including:

- a deep 20cm square one for French Fancies
- a shallow 20cm square one for Ginger Blondies
- 2 x 20cm sandwich tins for Victoria sandwiches
- 2 x 18cm sandwich tins (optional)
- a 12-hole muffin tray for cupcakes and muffins
- a 12- or 24-hole mini muffin tray for mini muffins and cupcakes
- a 23cm springform cake tin
- a rectangular baking/cake tin.

Light aluminium cake tins tend to bake more slowly and result in lighter-coloured crusts than dark cake tins, which bake faster. If you have dark-coloured cake tins, reduce the baking temperature of your recipe by 10°C.

Digital kitchen scales (baking is precise, digital scales will make everything easier).

Digital thermometer (for sugar, for jam, for everything).

Microplane grater (for zesting and grating).

Mixing bowl.

Offset palette knife.

Palette knife (for smooth application of icing and buttercream).

Paper cupcake, muffin and mini muffin cases, good-quality ones – it's easier to ice cupcakes using the edge of the cases and a palette knife.

Parchment paper (or silicone paper) is better than greaseproof paper for a non-stick surface. Or buy silicone mats, such as Silpats.

Pastry brushes: I have both silicone and natural fibre. Silicone is more heatproof but natural fibres (the Rosle brand is good) apply liquid more consistently. But make sure the bristles don't fall out easily. Stay away from nylon; it melts.

Piping/icing bags and piping nozzles/tips: see under Decorating Tools (see opposite page).

Rolling pin.

Set of measuring spoons: but do check that these are accurate as the capacity of the same spoon can vary. A teaspoon is 5ml/5g and a tablespoon is 15ml/15g. All spoon measurements are level, not heaped, unless the recipe states otherwise.

Sieve.

Silicone spatula (or several) for stirring, scraping, smoothing – I use these for absolutely everything.

Small, sharp knife.

Sugar thermometer (or digital thermometer – see left) for sugar work.

Tea strainer.

Vegetable peeler.

Wire cooling rack (a couple would be useful).

Wooden spoons.

Optional: **Rolling pin 'guides'** (these are a pro baker's gadget, very cheap, about £3.50. They are thin plastic rods, about 3–5mm in depth, which are placed either side of your dough and your rolling pin rests upon them; this ensures that the dough you are rolling out is very flat and even all over). They are especially useful for biscuits.

A Word of Advice about Baking

Here are my best tips for baking. I'd like you to buy some basic equipment that will make life so much easier, and your baking even better.

Decorating Cakes

This is a skill in itself. I've had beautifully decorated cakes that didn't taste particularly good. The ideal is to balance the two skills: content and form. In the West Indies, women often bake their own cakes, say for their daughter's wedding, but will go to a local lady, often a neighbour, who then decorates and ices their cake.

Decorating Tools

Food colouring: buy professional food colouring pastes rather than liquids, the colours are so much stronger and the packets last longer as you don't need to use very much.

Piping/icing bags: I almost always use large blue catering disposable piping bags that are called 'savoy'. These are easy to grip and not slippery like so many 'amateur' piping bags. They are, however, rather large, but this doesn't really matter, you just push however much of what you are using down to the bottom of the bag, and if you are doing fine work, cut off a small amount of the tip and insert, if using, a nozzle. Lakeland (and other suppliers) also do smaller disposable piping bags that are sold in smaller quantities. Alternatively, you can use a clean ziplock bag for piping icing (with the tip cut off a bottom corner), if you prefer.

Piping nozzles/tips: if you are going to become an expert decorator, then you will need a full array of icing nozzles. But generally I don't use them unless I want a specific shape such as a star. Icing sugar is cheap, so practise! Cakes are mostly curved, so practise on a wine glass.

Basic nozzles: a small round (plain) nozzle for piping straight lines and a star-shaped one should be sufficient. Wilton's 1M nozzle is the one to use for cupcake buttercream swirls (see stockists on page 250).

Oven Basics

My temperatures are given in centigrade and gas. If you have a fan-assisted oven, lower the temperature by 20°C. I use a 3-oven Aga. Most baking I do is in the baking oven. For those of you who have 2-oven Agas, most of the recipes can be baked in the roasting oven with the cold shelf.

Do calibrate your oven. Get a cheap oven thermometer, whack up your oven to the highest temperature, leave it for 30 minutes and then check the temperature. If the temperature is above or below what it should be, take this into account with all recipes.

Most ovens have hot spots, so I recommend turning trays of biscuits and buns around halfway through baking. Get to know your oven. Does it bake evenly at the same temperature? Cakes should generally be baked on the middle shelf of the oven (though with fan-assisted ovens this is less relevant as the temperature should be even throughout the oven).

My advice is to invest, if you can possibly afford it, in a great oven, preferably gas. It will last for decades and you will become a better baker for it.

Preparing Your Cake Tin

Important and basic. You can use specially shaped parchment paper inserts (available from kitchenware and baking supply shops). This is an especially good idea with a deeper cake. Or, you can grease the inside of the tin with butter, then sift flour through a tea strainer all over the bottom and inside edges, and tap out any excess. In the war, when butter was scarce due to rationing, they used to save butter papers for this purpose. If you are making a chocolate cake, you can sift chocolate powder or unsweetened cocoa powder over the inside.

Do this before you prepare your cake batter.

After Baking

Leave the cake to cool in the tin for at least 10 minutes (but depending on the recipe, it might be longer), then remove it carefully and place it on a wire rack. Cool your cake right side up! If it gets stuck in the tin, briefly heat the bottom of the cake tin with a blowtorch or by placing it on top of a tea towel soaked in boiling water. This will loosen the bottom.

Baking Terms

Most of you will know these, but I have a teenage daughter who proves that not everybody does know! This government says they are bringing back domestic science into schools. It's not a moment too soon.

Bain-marie (also known as a water bath): a French term for the technique of, say, melting chocolate in a bowl set over a pan of gently simmering or hot water. You'll need a heatproof bowl that fits over a pan, leaving enough room underneath the bowl to put water in the pan, BUT the bowl **must not** touch the simmering water underneath. You also cook some custards and certain cakes (cheesecakes) in a bain-marie.

Beat: stirring vigorously with a wooden spoon/spatula or the beater attachment on a stand mixer set at a medium speed. The idea is to simultaneously smooth the mixture and get air into it so that your cakes will be lighter. Beat eggs in slowly (at a lower speed), either one by one, or ideally, in even smaller amounts gradually, until each amount of egg is completely incorporated and the mixture doesn't curdle. Some bakers say that, if the mixture does start to split, add a teaspoon of flour, beat, then continue with the eggs. Others disagree and think beating the flour in makes the end result tougher.

Cream: mostly you are creaming together sugar and softened butter. You are trying to add air to your mixture and achieve a smooth, creamy consistency. Do this for at least 10 minutes. Longer than you think.

Cut in: a pastry-making term whereby you use a pastry cutter or two round-bladed knives to chop butter into flour.

Fold: using a thin metal spoon or rubber spatula to gently flop the mixture over itself in a figure-of-eight motion. You are not stirring vigorously as that would deflate the air. Much of good baking is about trying to retain air in the mixture.

Knead: with bread this is a pushing forward then pulling back motion with the dough. Kneading takes practice but is very important for getting elasticity into breads and buns. Knead until you have a 'window', that is, when you hold a piece of dough up to the light and, when you pull it apart, the gluten has been activated to the point that the dough forms a transparent, window-like section.

Overprove: when you've left the dough too long and it rises, then sinks. Try not to do this!

Prove: leaving a dough mixture to rise (usually in a warm place).

Scrape down: scraping the mixture down from the sides of the bowl to incorporate all the ingredients into the mixture.

Stir: mixing with a spoon using a *circular* movement. Yes, it's different from folding.

Whip: using a whisk to incorporate air into, say, cream.

Whisk: a whisk adds air as you mix ingredients together.

Soft peaks: the mixture (mostly eggs and sugar, also cream) forms a floppy peak. It still looks quite matt.

Firm peaks: the peaks hold well but the tips flop over.

Stiff peaks: the mixture forms a fairly rigid (and for meringues) quite glossy peak.

Is it cooked?: test cakes by inserting a fine skewer into the centre – if it emerges clean, then the cake is cooked. If it emerges with any uncooked mixture on, then the cake is not quite ready and should be baked a little longer (unless the cake is, say, a gooey chocolate cake or brownies). Another technique is to lightly press the centre of the cake with your finger and if the cake springs back up, then it's done.

About Sugar

A quick lowdown on sugar and how to cook with it.

There are two types of sugar: cane (a type of grass) and beet (like a big white beetroot that, when processed, produces sugar). Many bakers prefer cane sugar as they say it browns better to give a superior finish, but both do the job. There are also other sweeteners you can use: honey, maple syrup and agave syrup, for example.

Sugar is a fascinating product. Surprisingly, it contains a large amount of water, it is flexible, and it has several different 'flavours' and not just a generic sweetness. It's good to learn about all the different sugars and what they are best used for.

From Light to Dark: the Sugars

Type of Sugar	Grain Size / Texture	Best Used For
Granulated	Bog standard, large-grained white sugar.	Sweetening tea and coffee, making mulled wine, sprinkling over cakes and biscuits for decoration.
Caster	Finely ground white sugar.	Meringues, general baking and desserts.
Icing or golden icing (see opposite page)	Very finely ground, powdered white sugar.	Icings: royal, glacé, buttercream, fondant, ready-to-roll.
Soft brown, light or dark	White caster sugar with molasses added.	Fruit cakes, flapjacks.
Muscovado, light or dark	Unrefined brown sugar from Barbados.	Fruit cakes.
Demerara	Fruity brown sugar from Guyana with large glassy granules.	Dark cakes, such as fruit cakes, and crunchy toppings.
Molasses	A by-product of sugar-refining.	Rich fruit cakes, gingerbread, toffee. Rich in iron.
Honey	Double the sweetness of sugar and burns more easily.	Honey has a strong flavour. Breads, cakes, biscuits; for drizzling.
Invert sugars	Syrups, such as golden syrup, liquid glucose and light corn syrup.	Crystallisation prevention in cooking. Golden syrup can also be used in baking and desserts.

Sugar Work

Please buy a sugar thermometer or a digital thermometer. It's essential for all sugar work and is a generally useful thing to have for your cooking.

Sugar temperature is very important when making sweets and a thermometer will help to make those recipes a great deal easier. The higher the temperature of sugar, the harder it will set.

One of the things to watch out for is the dreaded 'crystallisation'. Have you ever seen jars of jam that have started to return to a crunchy, sugary state? This is because sugar prefers to be in crystallised rather than liquid form, so even one little unliquified crystal will attract the other sugar molecules. To avoid this problem:

- Keep the lid on the pan: moisture will form inside, dripping down the inside of the pan.
- Or, keep brushing around the top of the inside of the pan with a heatproof pastry brush dipped in water.
- Do not stir until all the crystals are melted, otherwise they will clag together.

Different Icings

There are several different kinds of icing sugar. Ignore all that. You want plain icing sugar. If you want to make royal icing, there is a simple recipe (see below).

Buttercream: (for cupcakes, big cakes, sandwich cakes) beat 150g softened unsalted butter until light and fluffy, then gradually stir in 300g icing sugar, a few drops of vanilla extract and a few drops of milk and beat until smooth and combined.

Glacé: (for éclairs) mix icing sugar with a little hot water.

Royal: (dries hard, used on biscuits and in wedding cakes) mix together 250g icing sugar, 1 egg white and a few drops of lemon juice until smooth. If you are piping it, divide the icing into several small airtight containers so that it doesn't dry out.

Fondant: (a glucose icing used for French Fancies) buy in packs and melt it in a bain-marie (see page 69).

Fondant icing is increasingly an area of contention. In America 'fondant icing' is simply ready-to-roll icing. This is very confusing, as many UK outlets have adopted this American terminology. Ready-to-roll fondant icing doesn't taste very nice. But if the pack says 'ready-to-roll' it's not proper fondant, you can't roll fondant. Genuine fondant icing must be bought from a specialist: it's a meltable icing that gives you a glossy smooth look.

Another tip: don't buy a box of (famous brand) powdered icing sugar with the words 'fondant' on it. This is not fondant either.

You can make real fondant yourself but it's a faff, so just order it.

Sugar syrup: (baste over the top of a cake or cupcakes before icing – a pro baker's trick to make sure your cakes stay moist) make a standard sugar syrup with a 1:1 ratio, e.g. 100g caster/granulated sugar and 100ml water.

About Flour

A note about flour and sifting. In the old days, it was important to sift flour, to get rid of lumps and weevils. Nowadays, most flour is free of both. We sift flour to introduce air into it. If the flour doesn't really need sifting, then aerate the flour by whisking it with a fork or balloon whisk or with the whisk in a stand mixer, for a minute or so. Same with icing sugar: I tend not to sift it unless it is lumpy or hard; I just aerate it with a fork, checking for lumps.

How to Work with Pastry

- Chill and 'rest' your pastry before working with it.
- I press pastry into flat discs, covered with cling film, to make rolling out easier.
- When rolling out, dust with flour underneath the pastry only to begin with.
- Flour your work surface with a light movement, as if throwing pebbles which skim across the top of the water.
- Work quickly as pastry starts to soften and become sticky.
- As the pastry warms, you can flour your rolling pin a little.
- Keep your hands cool. Professional pastry chefs often keep a bowl of iced water next to them, in which to dip (then dry) their hands, should they become too warm.
- Try not to use too much flour when working with pastry, as this will change the ratio of your ingredients. You can end up adding 50% more flour than the recipe states, if you're not careful.
- Use rolling pin 'guides' if necessary to maintain an even thickness of rolling. These are thin plastic rods, about 3–5mm in depth, which are placed onto either side of your dough, and your rolling pin rests upon them.
- When making pastry circles, roll from the middle away from you.
- Turn the pastry in quarter turns after each roll.

Flours and Raising Agents

Type	More Info / Texture	Best Used For
Plain	Standard flour, try to buy organic or local if you have a mill near you.	Most cooking purposes, cakes, pastry, general baking.
Strong/bread	Higher gluten content than plain flour.	Bread.
Self-raising	Plain flour with baking powder added: it rises.	Cakes, biscuits.
Type '00'	Very soft, fine, white Italian flour.	Pasta, some biscuits and pastry.
Spelt	Spelt is an ancient relative of modern wheat; the grain is a variety of wheat: high protein, lower fibre and easier to digest than wheat, lots of flavour, does contain some gluten.	Popular in Scandinavian baking, speciality breads and pastry.
Rye	Non-wheat flour, contains gluten, high protein.	Good for making sourdough starters and for mixing with wheat flour for richer/dense breads.
Buckwheat	Gluten-free, dark, flavoursome, sour, nutty taste.	Good for blinis and pancakes.
Gluten-free	You can buy this in various types, including plain or self-raising white flour, brown or white bread flour; made from blends of gluten-free flours, such as rice, potato, tapioca, maize and buckwheat. Gluten-free dough is more difficult to knead and shape.	Use as substitute for wheat flour in many recipes, including cakes, bakes and some breads.
Rice flour	Finely ground rice, gluten-free, light.	Used for Asian baking, such as Vietnamese baguettes, cakes.
Cornflour	A thickener. Don't confuse with cornmeal. Gluten-free.	Custards, sauces.
Cornmeal	Thicker, rougher and harder than cornflour, like polenta. Gluten-free.	Adds crunch to baking, can be used to make tortillas.
Bicarbonate of soda	Raising agent, use quickly, has a bitter flavour.	Honeycomb, biscuits, soda bread.
Baking powder	Raising agent, ready-mixed bicarbonate of soda and cream of tartar.	Most cake recipes, some quick breads.
Cream of tartar	A stabiliser (acid).	Meringues (for chewy centres), whipped cream, icing.

Pastry

Type of Pastry	*Best Used In*
Pâte sucrée/sweet shortcrust	Sweet tarts. Pliable.
Pâte à choux/choux	Éclairs, gougères, puffs, profiteroles, doughnuts. You cook it in a pan. Easy.
Pâte sablée/biscuit dough	Biscuits. A higher sugar content so it has 'snap'. Hard to roll out so press into tart tins.
Pâte brisée/shortcrust/fractured dough	Savoury tarts. Retains bits of butter or oil in the dough, which gives it a crumbly texture. No sugar.
Pâte feuilletée/puff or flaky	Croissants. Takes hours. Worth a go though.
Filo; don't bother making this at home, it's too hard	Baklava, tartlets/parcels.
Hot-water crust, not difficult	Raised pies.

Baking Blind

When you are filling a tart with an uncooked filling, the pastry needs to be fully baked before the filling is added. Line your tin with pastry, then prick the bottom of the pastry shell all over with a fork so that it doesn't bubble up. Line the pastry shell with a sheet of greaseproof paper, then fill it with baking beans or special clay beads (or use some dried pulses). Bake as directed. Once it is nearly cooked, remove the beans and paper and bake for a few more minutes until fully cooked.

Eggs

Use medium, unless the recipe states otherwise.

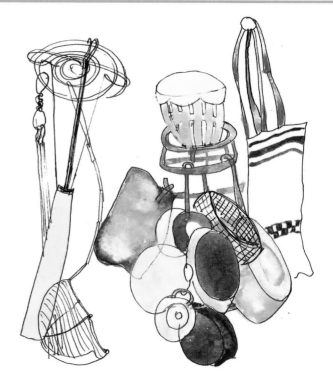

About Yeast

Yeast is a raising agent, used for some of the savoury and sweet recipes in this book. But, there are several different types, which can cause confusion. I keep all my yeast, fresh or dried, in the fridge. Keep an eye on the 'use-by' date, you want to make sure it is alive and kicking.

Do not add too much yeast to make the proving 'go faster'. Your baked goods will not have a pleasant taste. Add just the right amount.

Yeast loves sugar and doesn't like salt. When mixing doughs, try to keep yeast a little apart from the salt, which slows down the proving (rising).

Do not mix yeast with hot water, it will kill the organisms which you need to make your dough rise. The water (or other liquid) should never be hotter than lukewarm.

When mixing yeast with milk, to make doughs such as brioche, yeast will act more slowly. Be patient.

Yeast	
Type of Yeast	*Best Used In*
Fresh yeast	Not widely available, though some bakers and delis stock it and it is available online. Usually comes in little 42g squares. Keep in the fridge or even the freezer as it has a short shelf life. Use triple the amount of fresh yeast that you would for dried yeast (instant or active), e.g. 7g of dried yeast would be 21g of fresh yeast. Professional bakers swear by it, but for the home cook, dried yeast is more convenient for smaller quantities of baking.
Fast–action or Instant dried yeast/ Easy–bake or Easy–blend dried yeast/Rapid Rise dried yeast	The most popular kind. Often available in 7g sachets. Does not need to be activated in water, can be added straight to the flour.
Dried yeast/Active dry yeast	Needs to be activated in lukewarm water and a little sugar or honey (for 10 minutes or so, until a frothy head appears on top) before adding to the flour and other ingredients.
Brewer's yeast	This is used in beer and wine. Can be used for making fizzy soft drinks. Champagne yeast is less bitter and has a more unobtrusive flavour. Can be bought in pharmacies as a health–food supplement, full of vitamin B.
Wild yeast	Before commercial yeast, we had wild yeast, which relies on the invisible spores of airborne yeasts in the atmosphere, to raise baked goods, specifically sourdough (we still use this for making sourdough today). Has a lovely flavour but takes time to rise. You can cheat a little by using commercial yeast, but leaving it to ferment longer so the dough has a slightly sour taste (many of us like this!). Naturally risen and proved dough is very good for the flora and fauna of your gut.

Biscuits

Ginger Biscuits (*Pepperkakor*)

Makes 30

180g soft dark brown sugar
4–5 tbsp golden syrup
2 tbsp orange juice
2 tbsp ground cinnamon
2 tbsp ground ginger
½ tsp ground cloves
A pinch of sea salt
200g unsalted butter, diced
1 tsp bicarbonate of soda
450g plain flour, plus extra for dusting
1 quantity (250g) royal icing (see page 71)
   for decorating, divided and kept in
   small airtight containers

EQUIPMENT
A selection of Christmassy biscuit cutters

*Biscuits need to be kept in a cool,
dry place. Store biscuits in an airtight
container for up to 2 weeks.*

These Swedish biscuits are great to bake for Christmas decorations, either for the table or for hanging from a tree. Just punch a little hole in each biscuit and thread a ribbon through it.

Put the sugar, golden syrup, orange juice, cinnamon, ginger, cloves and salt into a pan over a medium heat and bring to the boil while stirring, then take the pan off the heat and stir in the butter. Once combined, add the bicarbonate of soda and whisk. Pour this mixture into the bowl of a stand mixer and leave to cool until it is lukewarm.

Sift the flour over the top of the mixture and combine on low speed using the paddle attachment until it forms a dough. Wrap the dough in cling film and chill it in the fridge for 2 hours.

Line a baking sheet with parchment paper or a silicone mat. Place the chilled dough on a lightly floured surface and knead briefly, then, if you have bought rolling pin 'guides' (5mm ones), roll it to an even thickness (or simply roll out evenly to a thickness of 5mm). When making biscuits (or the Gingerbread Cottage on page 172), it's very important to roll out evenly, for if the edges are thinner and middles thicker, the edges may burn.

Use the Christmassy biscuit cutters to cut out the shapes. If you want to use them as hanging ornaments, make a hole 1.5cm from the top of each biscuit in which to thread the ribbon or twine later. Make the holes a little larger than you think because they will close up as the biscuits bake. Using a palette knife, lay these on the prepared baking sheet. Chill again for 30 minutes.

Preheat the oven to 200°C (gas 6).

Bake the biscuits for 10–12 minutes, until golden brown, then lift off the sheet, carefully, and leave to cool on a wire rack.

When they have cooled, ice them with the royal icing (see page 79) and leave to dry for at least 24 hours before storing in an airtight container, eating them or hanging them on your tree.

Biscuit Labels

Use the biscuit dough recipe from the Ruby Shoe Biscuits recipe on page 194 to make these. Roll out the dough, then using a template, cut out label shapes. Insert a hole in each one for the ribbon before you bake them. Once baked and cooled, pipe the names of your guests on to the labels in royal icing (see opposite) and tie them to the teacup handles using pretty ribbons.

How to Pipe Royal Icing

his is a skill you will need for piping biscuits or gingerbread houses. You can buy disposable piping/icing bags or a professional fabric one and insert different nozzles inside the bag. It's something that requires practice but here are some useful tips. The basic Royal Icing recipe can be found on page 71.

Making

It's important to get the consistency of the icing just right; to pipe well it needs to be runny but also hold its shape, not too chalky but not too liquid.

Add more lemon juice if the icing starts to dry up, or when you need a looser consistency to fill or flood biscuits.

Edging and flooding require two different consistencies of icing: stiffer for the edging and more liquid for the flooding.

As soon as you've made your batch of icing, it's advisable to divide it into several small airtight containers to prevent the whole lot drying up as you work.

Piping

To fill a piping/icing bag, first stand it in a tall jug, then fold down the sides to hold it in place while you pour in the icing.

Pipe the outline first, using a stiffer icing and a thinner nozzle in your piping/icing bag.

Make a dot of icing on the biscuit to act as an anchor then lift the tip and lasso the icing to the next 'point'. Make another anchoring dot before moving on.

To test the consistency of icing for flooding, blob some of the icing on to a surface and run a knife through the middle. If it takes less than 10 seconds for the gap to close then it is too runny. You don't want it to close too slowly, either.

Don't stop once you start flooding the biscuit, just keep going.

Finishing

Ideally icing needs to be left overnight to dry properly so that you could, if desired, pipe another layer. You want the icing to set really hard.

Button Biscuits

Makes 20-25

85g unsalted butter, softened
50g cream cheese
100g caster sugar
½ tsp vanilla extract
275g plain flour, plus extra for dusting
1 small egg, beaten
½ tsp baking powder
¼ tsp sea salt
Food colouring pastes of your choice

EQUIPMENT
4cm round biscuit cutter
3cm round biscuit cutter
Small round piping nozzle

I spent my early years living above a haberdasher's shop in Hull. There is something fantastical and storybook-like about haberdashers with their coils of ribbon, trim, appliqués, pincushions, patches, cottons and buttons. Along with hardware shops, haberdashers are among my favourite places for treasure hunts.

The comedian Michael McIntyre talks about the 'man drawer' in every home that's full of batteries, foreign coins and instruction booklets. Surely we have the equivalent 'woman drawer', a place *The Borrowers* would delight in making use of, containing a decorative litter of buttons, odd earrings and safety pins.

In a bowl, beat together the butter, cream cheese, sugar and vanilla extract until light and fluffy.

In another bowl, combine half of the flour and the egg. Add the rest of the flour, the baking powder and salt. Add this mixture to the butter mixture and combine until you have a soft dough.

Divide this dough into halves or quarters and tint each portion with a different food colour (gently work the food colouring paste into the dough until it is evenly incorporated). Wrap in cling film and chill in the fridge for 2 hours.

Line a baking sheet with parchment paper or a silicone mat.

Remove one of the dough pieces from the fridge and roll it out on a lightly floured work surface so that it is just over 1cm thick. Cut out small rounds with the 4cm cutter, then make a light indentation using the 3cm cutter to create a border just in from the edge, without pushing through the dough. Then, with the small round piping nozzle, cut 2 or 4 holes in the centre of each biscuit so that it resembles a button, making sure to push down to the counter so that the small pieces fall out. Lift the biscuits on to the prepared baking sheet and refrigerate for 15 minutes. Repeat with the other pieces of coloured dough.

Meanwhile, preheat the oven to 180°C (gas 4).

Bake the biscuits for 8–10 minutes or until it looks as if the edges might start to brown. At that point, immediately remove them from the oven, as you want to preserve their pastel colours. Transfer to a wire rack and leave to cool.

Nice Arse Biscuits

I met Emma Beddington on Twitter: she's @belgianwaffling. She came to sell her 'arse' biscuits at one of my Underground Farmers Markets and sold out very quickly.

'I'm a freelance writer based in Belgium with a great love of baked goods. My then seven–year–old son Louis discovered a Brigitte Keks printing set in a local toyshop and set his strange, orderly heart upon it. As soon as we got it home and out of the packet, the potential for subversive biscuitry was immediately apparent. When Louis went to bed I started experimenting with his new toy and came up with a set of very rude, but also dainty and delicate biscuits, which I posted on my blog. They instantly caught the imagination of my similarly childish readers and a (small, unsuccessful) business was born. With my best friend Madevi, we created Cruel Tea, a range of rude word–based teatime requisites: not only biscuits, but also tea cosies, fridge magnets and aprons, which we continue to sell with very little success on Etsy. Arse Biscuits are perfect served on a fine china plate with a lovely pot of leaf tea, to a short–sighted elderly relative. (PS: I did eventually buy my own set of cutters and give Louis his toy back.)'

MsMarmiteLover says: I know readers will want to try this recipe. I used the same one to make 'rich tea' biscuits, using a scalloped cutter and prodding holes in pretty patterns. Here, I've added desiccated coconut to give the flavour, as well as the appearance, of Nice biscuits.

Makes 30–40

*175g salted butter, softened (or use
  unsalted butter and add ½ tsp sea salt)*
200g caster sugar
2 large eggs, beaten
*1 tsp of any flavouring/extract you wish:
  vanilla, almond, lemon…*
400g plain flour, plus extra for dusting
½ tsp baking powder
100g desiccated coconut

EQUIPMENT
*A Brigitte Keks biscuit-printing set
  (available online – see stockists on
  page 250)*

*Note from MsMarmiteLover: dip the cutter
in flour before cutting out each biscuit, this
way dough will not get stuck in it.*

In a bowl, cream together the butter and sugar until pale in colour, then beat in the eggs and flavouring. Sift the flour and baking powder into the mixture, then add the desiccated coconut. Mix slowly until it forms a ball of dough.

Divide the dough in half, roll each half into a ball, wrap both balls in cling film and chill in the fridge for at least 30 minutes. These 30 minutes are the ideal time to decide what words you want to print on your biscuits. The Brigitte Keks printing set is easy to use but fiddly, with tiny letters likely to escape all over your kitchen. I sort them on a tray for easy reference. Fit your chosen letters into the cutter – short (four letter!) words look better, I find – and ensure they are centred. For sanity's sake, I try to stick to one or two words per batch of biscuits, but you may be more patient than me!

Preheat the oven to 180°C (gas 4). Line a baking sheet with parchment paper or a silicone mat.

Remove one of the balls of dough from the fridge and roll it out on a well-floured surface to around 5mm thickness. Take your time over this stage because it is crucial – if the dough is unevenly rolled, your biscuit won't have that neat, plump surface that is the perfect foil for your rude word.

Cut out biscuits with the cutter. You need to cut, then depress the plunger thingy on the top of the cutter just enough to get the word well printed – you'll probably need a few practice tries to get this right. Once you've got the hang of it (be ruthless, if they don't look quite right raw, they'll look terrible cooked), use a palette knife to transfer the finished biscuits to the prepared baking sheet. You want the flattest surface possible for an even rise.

Put the first batch in the oven and bake for around 8–12 minutes, until golden brown around the edges. Transfer to a wire rack to cool. Repeat with the second ball of dough.

Giant Custard Cream Jammie Dodger

Makes 1 large jammie dodger/
Serves 8–10

250g unsalted butter, softened
140g icing sugar
1 tsp vanilla extract, or 1 vanilla pod split
   in half lengthways and seeds scraped out
1 large egg yolk
A pinch of sea salt
375g plain flour, sifted
30g caster sugar, for sprinkling

FOR THE FILLING
150g icing sugar
75g unsalted butter, softened
2 tbsp custard powder
170g seedless raspberry
   or blackcurrant jam

These days it seems everybody is doing a recipe for jammie dodgers, named after Roger the Dodger from *The Beano*. But mine has custard cream in it and it's big, like a cake. I made smaller blackcurranty ones for my *Dr Who*-themed meal. The 11th doctor used a jammie dodger as a psychological weapon against the Daleks.

You can, of course, use this same recipe to make small jammie dodgers. If you are making small ones, you'll need a smaller cutter to cut out the centre of half of your biscuits before baking (a heart-shaped cutter works well), these will form the top of your 'sandwiched pairs of biscuits. You could also use a larger heart-shaped cutter for the top biscuit layer of the giant jammie dodger, if you like.

Place the butter and icing sugar in a bowl and beat together with an electric whisk for 1 minute, until smooth, pale and fluffy. Add the vanilla extract or seeds, egg yolk and salt and then gradually beat in the flour to make a smooth dough. Wrap the dough in cling film and chill in the fridge for an hour.

Preheat the oven to 190°C (gas 5).

Cut the chilled dough in half and place each half on a sheet of parchment paper or a silicone mat. Roll them out into circles of the same size, about 20cm in diameter and 5mm thick. Use rolling pin 'guides' if you have them. Cut a large hole from the centre of one biscuit.

Slide the paper or mats on to 2 baking sheets and bake for about 23 minutes, until pale golden. Turn the baking sheets around halfway through baking in case of hotspots, and if cooking on two shelves, then swap the sheets around too. Carefully transfer to a wire rack to cool. Sprinkle caster sugar over the biscuit with the hole while it is still warm so the sugar caramelises a bit.

Once cool, place the plain biscuit layer on to a flat serving plate or cake stand.

For the filling, beat together the icing sugar, butter and custard powder until smooth and combined, then use a spatula to spread the custard cream in a layer over the bottom biscuit layer. Spread a layer of jam on top, then place the sugar-sprinkled biscuit layer on top.

Cut into wedges to serve.

Chocolate Cannoli

Makes 22, serves 6? Ha!

300g type '00' pasta flour
120g plain flour, plus extra for dusting
55g caster sugar
15g good-quality unsweetened cocoa powder
10g sea salt
½ tsp a mixture of finely ground cinnamon and cloves
    (optional: grains of paradise)
30g solid vegetable fat, such as Trex or lard
40g unsalted butter
2 eggs, beaten
100g Marsala or sweet sherry
1 tsp balsamic vinegar
1 tsp vanilla extract
400g good-quality white cooking chocolate,
    broken into pieces
3–4 tbsp ground toasted almonds or hazelnuts, or freeze-
    dried raspberry powder (available at Waitrose or online)
Crystallised rose petals (optional)
Egg wash, for sealing
Sunflower or corn oil, for deep-frying

FOR THE FILLING
20g freeze-dried raspberry powder
75ml good rose water (I find Middle Eastern the best,
    English rose water seems too light and lacks the
    perfumed whack I'm after)
15g Chambord raspberry liqueur, or use crème de
    framboise, crème de myrtille or crème de cassis
1kg ricotta, drained (very important)
265g icing sugar

FOR THE RASPBERRY SHERBET
DUST (OPTIONAL):
2 tsp vanilla caster sugar
2 tsp freeze-dried raspberry powder
¼ tsp citric acid or a 5g sachet of Fizz Wiz
    (available online)

EQUIPMENT
Cannoli moulds/tubes
Pastry brush (I favour silicone to avoid bristles ending up
    in the chocolate)
Piping bag fitted with a large star-shaped nozzle

Tony Cannoli has a name that could come straight out of *The Sopranos* but he actually hails from north-east London. He sells his Sicilian Italian pastries, cannoli, at markets in London through his small food business, The Hungry Wolf Ltd. He's kindly sent me his interesting cannoli recipe.

There are simple recipes in this book and the odd challenging one to stretch your skills. Some-times, even within a traditional English tea party, you want something a little more exotic. Set aside half a day for this recipe and have a go!

Traditionally cannoli are fried pastries stuffed with a sweet ricotta-based cream, with a hint of orange-blossom water, a few bitter chocolate chips and pieces of crystallised fruit at the ends. The *cialde* (Italian for wafers) are deep-fried, wrapped around a metal core or, for the more old-school, a length of thick bamboo. Traditionally, highly refined lard (*strutto*) is used for the dough, but for a wider public Tony tends to use a mixture of butter and vegetable fat. He finds that butter alone does not give the right texture.

Tony adds: 'I love traditional cannoli but have enjoyed experimenting. I've made all sorts of different flavours, made creams based on mascarpone instead of ricotta, even a vegan one using silken tofu as the cream base. The core of the cannoli experience for me is a shattering and crumbly shell that yields into something rich, creamy, sweet and gorgeous! Overleaf is the recipe for raspberry and rose-flavoured cannoli (see picture on pages 88–89), which has been a firm favourite with family and customers. My variation is to make a thinner dough and coat it with a liberal layer of melted good chocolate: plain for some flavours, white for the one here. Some favour different types of milk chocolate. For the raspberry and rose-flavoured cannoli, I also give the tops a good splatter of melted chocolate, stick a crystallised rose petal on top of each one, dip the ends in toasted kibbled almonds and dust with sour raspberry sherbet.'

In a large bowl, thoroughly mix together the two flours, caster sugar, cocoa powder, salt and ground spices. Add the vegetable fat and butter and rub in until the mixture resembles breadcrumbs.

In a separate bowl, mix together the eggs, Marsala or sherry, balsamic vinegar and vanilla extract and add to the dry mix, bringing the dough together until you have a silky texture. Cover and leave to rest for 1 hour at room temperature, then knead again until silky.

Roll out the dough on a lightly floured work surface until it is 3mm thick. (If you have a pasta machine, work through the settings until thickness number 2, sprinkling the rollers with flour.) Use saucers as templates to cut out circles that will fit your cannoli moulds and wrap the circles around the moulds. Use a little egg wash to moisten the overlap.

If you have a deep-fat fryer, preheat it to 160°C. If not, use a deep pan or wok, filling it with a good few centimetres of clean sunflower or corn oil that hasn't been used for anything savoury, and heat it to 160°C. The oil is hot enough when a cube of bread sizzles when it hits the oil and turns golden within 20 seconds.

Deep-fry the cannoli for 5 minutes or until golden brown and knobbly in appearance. You will have to fry them in batches depending how many cannoli moulds you have. Remove the moulds from the oil with tongs, letting the moulds drip any excess oil back into the fryer. Leave to cool on a wire rack, then carefully remove the cannoli from the moulds and then wrap the next batch of cannoli around the moulds. Repeat until all the cannoli are cooked.

Melt the white chocolate in a bain-marie (see page 69), making sure the bowl doesn't touch the simmering water underneath, or melt it in a bowl in the microwave (on full power) in short 30-second bursts, then paint the insides of the cannoli shells with melted chocolate using a pastry brush. Dip the ends of the cannoli in the chocolate, then into ground nuts or freeze-dried raspberry powder. Set aside to dry, then drizzle the tops with any remaining melted chocolate and adhere a crystallised rose petal to the top of each one, if you wish.

To make the filling, moisten the freeze-dried raspberry powder in a small bowl with the rose water and Chambord. In a larger bowl, thoroughly mix together the ricotta and icing sugar until smooth. Pour the liquids into the ricotta mixture and whip to a thick moussy texture. Transfer the ricotta cream to the piping bag and pipe it into the cannoli shells. Be generous.

If you wish, make the raspberry sherbet dust by thoroughly grinding all the ingredients together using a pestle and mortar. Dust the cannoli with the sherbet just before serving.

Chocolate-dipped Lemon and Almond Biscotti

Tip: You can mix a little of the lemon zest in with the melted chocolate, if you wish.

Makes 10–15 slices

150g plain flour
1½ tsp baking powder
100g caster sugar
2 small eggs, beaten
75g whole almonds,
   lightly toasted and coarsely chopped
Finely grated zest of 1 lemon
50g almond chocolate (good-quality dark or milk),
   roughly chopped

These are wonderful dipped into tea, hot chocolate or a liqueur.

Preheat the oven to 180°C (gas 4). Line a baking sheet with parchment paper or a silicone mat.

Mix together all the ingredients, except the almond chocolate, in a bowl to make a dough, then shape the dough into a flattish loaf. Transfer the loaf to the prepared baking sheet. Bake for 15 minutes or until golden.

Remove from the oven. Quickly cut the hot biscuit into slices and separate them out on the baking sheet. Return them to the oven for 5 minutes. Remove from the oven and leave them to cool on the baking sheet.

Melt the almond chocolate in a bain-marie (see page 69), making sure the bowl doesn't touch the simmering water underneath, or melt it in a bowl in the microwave (on full power) in short bursts – just in 30-second bursts at a time as you don't want the chocolate to seize up.

Dip half of each biscuit slice into the melted chocolate and then leave them to set on a clean sheet of parchment paper or a silicone mat.

Choux

Choux pastry is a cooked dough that puffs up when baked. It really isn't difficult to master.

Chouquettes

Makes 45

250ml water
100g unsalted butter
150g plain flour
1 tsp caster sugar
½ tsp sea salt
½ tsp fast-action dried yeast
A few drops of vanilla extract
3 large eggs, beaten
Nibbed sugar, for sprinkling

EQUIPMENT
Piping bag fitted with a wide plain nozzle
  (optional)

'Choux' means 'cabbage' in French; it's also used as a term of endearment – *mon petit chou* – between lovers, as in 'my little cabbage'. Doesn't work as well in translation, does it? Other French names for *les amants* include *ma crotte* 'my dropping', *mon cochon* 'my pig' and *ma biche* 'my (female) deer'. Let's face it, anything said in a French accent sounds romantic.

These are the lightest little teatime sugary puffs. So French, so frivolous, virtually a diet food. You can also fill them with crème pâtissière rather than stud them with nibbed sugar. This is the basic recipe used to make the Pastel Croquembouche on page 188, served as part of my Marie Antoinette Afternoon Tea.

Preheat the oven to 200°C (gas 6). Line a baking sheet with parchment paper or a silicone mat.

Heat up the water and butter in a pan until boiling. Once it's boiling, remove the pan from the heat and add, in one go, the flour, caster sugar, salt, yeast and vanilla extract. Stir with a wooden spoon until the dough starts to come away from the sides of the pan and becomes whole.

Gradually add the beaten eggs, incorporating each addition, until the dough fully absorbs the mixture. You could do this using an electric mixer.

Fill the piping bag with the dough and pipe out the chouquettes on to the prepared baking sheet (pipe small rounds about 3–4cm in diameter), or spoon a tablespoon of mixture for each one, leaving about 3cm space between each one to allow for expansion. Sprinkle over the nibbed sugar, pressing it lightly into the dough. Use plenty of nibbed sugar!

Bake for 30 minutes or until golden brown and crispy. Transfer to a wire rack to cool. Serve warm or cold.

Éclairs from the Dix Blue Secret Tea Room

Makes 20

125ml milk
125ml water
100g unsalted butter
½ tsp sea salt
1 tsp caster sugar
150g plain flour, sifted
4 eggs, beaten
1 beaten egg mixed with 1 tbsp milk,
    for glazing

FOR THE CARAMELISED
BANANA FILLING
4 large bananas
4 tbsp dark rum, white rum or brandy
65g caster sugar
1 tbsp unsalted butter
A heaped ½ tsp fleur de sel
    or Maldon sea salt
600ml double or whipping cream,
    whipped to firm peaks

FOR THE CHOCOLATE GLAZE
130g good-quality dark chocolate,
    broken into pieces
250ml water
125ml double cream
70g caster sugar

FOR THE YELLOW GLAZE
250g icing sugar
A few tsp boiling water
A few drops of banana essence (optional)
A little yellow food colouring paste

EQUIPMENT
3 piping bags, each fitted with a 2cm plain
    nozzle
1 piping bag, fitted with a large star-shaped
    nozzle

Have you made éclairs and struggled to make them look as professional as they do in cake shops? The glaze can look like a drippy mess. Shhh, I found out the secret: use the bottom for glazing. Yes, turn them over. You will have lovely straight lines.

I've made salted caramelised banana-filled éclairs here, inspired by Caroline Richardson who runs a secret tearoom called Dix Blue in Scotland (see page 249). You can make them in the shape of bananas with a yellow glaze, or the classic shape, glazed with chocolate. Caroline says, 'Think of these éclairs as banana boats, heavily laden with a cargo of fragrant, sweet and, not-un-nervingly, slightly salty fruitiness. The saltiness in the filling comes from the caramelisation of the bananas with the fleur de sel.'

For even baking, position two racks/shelves in the oven, one each in the upper and lower half, then preheat the oven to 180°C (gas 4). Line 2 baking sheets with parchment paper or silicone mats.

Bring the milk, water, butter, salt and caster sugar to the boil in a heavy-based pan over a medium-high heat, then remove from the heat and immediately dump the flour into the mixture, all in one go, stirring vigorously with a wooden spoon until all the flour is incorporated.

Gradually add the eggs, stirring rapidly until each addition is absorbed, then return the pan to a medium heat and continue to stir until the dough comes away from the sides of the pan and starts to 'dry' a little, but also becomes soft and smooth. Take the pan off the heat, leave the dough until it cools down, then transfer it into one of the piping bags with a plain nozzle. (The paste has to be warm to pipe well.)

(To save on elbow grease this step can be done in a stand mixer. Bring the milk, water, butter, salt and sugar to boil on the hob, then transfer the contents of the pan to the bowl of the mixer and quickly dump in the flour while the paddle is going. Then add the eggs one by one. Once the dough is smooth, soft and shiny, transfer it to the piping bag while still warm to the touch.)

Pipe the dough on to the prepared baking sheets in 10–15cm fingers. Or you can pipe curved banana shapes. Try to keep them even-sized so that they will look good once plated up. Once you've piped one out on the baking sheet, just follow that as your template.

Remember to leave about 5cm space in between each éclair to give them room to expand. Finally, get a cold fork dipped in cold water and run it over the top of each éclair – for some reason this makes them rise evenly. Brush the éclairs with the egg/milk glaze.

Pop the éclairs into the oven. Your total baking time will be 15–20 minutes, but set your timer for 7 minutes, then rotate the sheets so that the éclairs bake evenly, close the door and continue baking for a further 8 minutes or until the éclairs are a lovely tan colour and quite firm to the touch. Éclairs can turn from softly golden-topped to spray-tan Ibiza-bronze in literally seconds, so keep an eye on them. Once baked, transfer them to a wire rack, pierce the side of each one with the tip of a sharp knife (to allow the steam to escape and prevent them from going soggy) and leave to cool.

For the caramelised banana filling, chop the bananas into a medium-sized bowl and toss them in the rum/brandy. Set aside.

Make the caramel by heating a heavy-based pan over a medium-high heat. When it is warm and not too hot, sprinkle the caster sugar into the pan. Try to keep the sugar in an even layer so that it all caramelises at the same time. As soon as you see the sugar begin to melt, start moving the pan about – you need to avoid burning the sugar. A good way to do this and make sure you get an even caramel is to tilt the pan from side to side so that the melted sugar runs over the unmelted sugar. Cook until all of the sugar is a light golden brown. Any darker and it turns into toffee, so take care.

Move the pan off the heat, and then quickly stir in the butter and salt. Add the bananas and rum mixture, very carefully to avoid breaking up the bananas, and spread evenly in the pan. Return the pan to a medium heat until almost all of the liquid has evaporated and the bananas are soft but not mushy. Tip the caramelised bananas on to a plate. Cover with cling film and leave to cool for about 20 minutes.

For the chocolate glaze, put all the ingredients into a separate heavy-based pan over a medium heat and wait until the sauce thickens, stirring occasionally. Remove from the heat and allow it to cool slightly, then pour it into another piping bag with a plain nozzle. Turn the éclairs over and pipe a thick line of chocolate glaze over the top of half of the éclairs. Leave to dry for an hour or so before filling.

Meanwhile, for the yellow glaze, tip the icing sugar into a bowl and add, one by one, a few teaspoons of boiling water. Mix well until it forms a thick paste that you can pipe easily, but that doesn't run too much. Add a couple of drops of banana essence, if using, then the yellow colouring until it is the shade you desire. Pour the glaze into the remaining piping bag with a plain nozzle and pipe a thick line of yellow glaze over the top of the remaining éclairs. Leave to dry for an hour or so before filling.

When you are ready to serve, fold the cooled banana caramel into the whipped cream. Split the glazed éclairs and pipe in the banana cream.

Caroline suggests matching these with Orange Pekoe tea: 'Those mamby-pamby green teas just can't stand up to the full-frontal banana, boozy, sweet-salty flavour!'

Tips:
- *For alternative fillings, use plain whipped cream, or half whipped cream and half chocolate glaze (cooled) combined.*
- *If you have any leftover glazes, keep them in airtight containers in the fridge and use within a week.*

Tarts & Pies

Greengage Tart

Serves 8–10

200g plain flour, plus extra for dusting
A pinch of sea salt
110g unsalted butter, softened,
    plus extra for greasing
50g caster sugar
1 large egg, lightly beaten

FOR THE FILLING
100g unsalted butter, softened
100g caster sugar
2 eggs
100g ground almonds or hazelnuts
60g plain flour
500g greengages or other plums,
    halved and stoned

EQUIPMENT
20–23cm round loose-based tart tin
Baking beans or beads

In France they call greengage plums Reine Claude, after a particularly virtuous and popular queen from the Middle Ages, the wife of François I (who was around at the same time as our Henry VIII). Although her body was deformed by scoliosis, her inner beauty and sweet nature meant that Queen Claude was loved both by the people and by her husband ('he has never failed to sleep with her each night', which was quite unusual for a king). Anne Boleyn, the second (and beheaded) wife of Henry VIII, was part of her court for many years.

You can use this pastry recipe for any sweet or fruit tart.

Sift the flour and salt into a bowl.

In a separate bowl, cream the butter and mix in the sugar. Gradually add the beaten egg until incorporated, then tip the flour into the bowl in one go and mix until it forms a ball. Flatten the pastry into a disc, cover with cling film and leave it to rest in the fridge for 30 minutes.

Preheat the oven to 200°C (gas 6). Grease the tart tin, then use a tea strainer to sift a fine layer of flour over it, tipping out any excess.

Roll out the chilled pastry on a lightly floured work surface and press it into the bottom and up the sides of the prepared tart tin. Prick the bottom of the pastry all over with a fork, then line the pastry shell with a piece of greaseproof paper and cover the bottom with baking beans.

Bake for 15 minutes or until the crust is slightly golden. Remove from the oven, remove the beans and paper and leave the pastry shell to cool on a wire rack. Lower the oven temperature to 170°C (gas 3).

To make the filling, cream the butter and sugar together until pale and fluffy, then gradually mix in the eggs, one by one. Fold in the ground nuts and flour. Transfer the mixture to the cooled pastry shell, spreading it evenly, then arrange the greengage halves (cut sides down or up, it's your choice) in circles on top.

Bake for 30 minutes or until the filling is puffy and set. Serve warm.

Pastéis de Belém/Portuguese Custard Tarts

Makes 12

175ml milk
225ml double cream or crème fraîche
115g caster sugar
3 egg yolks
2 tbsp cornflour
½ tsp vanilla extract, lemon essence
  or pandan essence (see stockists on
  page 250, or you can make your own
  pandan essence, see page 218)
300g ready-made all-butter puff pastry
  (ready-rolled, if you like)
Unsalted butter, for greasing
Plain flour, for dusting

EQUIPMENT
12-hole muffin tray

I like to eat these at Café Lisboa, a tiny Portuguese café on Portobello Road in London. I was delighted to discover that they are easily made at home. The trick for the authentic light and layered pastry is to coil it up like a Swiss roll, then roll it out.

I made Pandan Custard Tarts for my Oriental-themed Afternoon Tea. The recipe is on page 218.

Put the milk and cream or crème fraîche into a pan and heat gently until almost boiling. Remove from the heat. In a heatproof bowl, whisk together the sugar, egg yolks, cornflour and flavouring. Gradually whisk in the hot milk mixture, then return the mixture to the pan and heat gently, stirring constantly, to make a custard. When you can draw a distinct line in the mixture with your wooden spoon, the custard is thick enough (do not overheat the mixture or allow it to boil at any stage, otherwise it will curdle). Remove from the heat, pour into a heatproof bowl, place a circle of parchment paper on the surface (to prevent a skin forming), and leave to cool.

Preheat the oven to 200°C (gas 6). Grease the holes of the muffin tray.

Roll out the puff pastry on a lightly floured work surface to 3mm thickness. To get all those lovely crispy, delicate layers that a Portuguese custard tart possesses, the proper way is to then roll your puff pastry up as if it were a Swiss roll and cut horizontal slices from your roll. Then, laying each slice horizontally, gently roll it out with a rolling pin to make a circle with a circumference big enough to fit the muffin tray holes, going up the sides as well. This forms the basis of your spirally custard tart. Tuck each pastry circle into a prepared muffin hole. If you've bought ready-made puff pastry in a sheet, just unroll it from the paper, reroll it and slice. Easy!

Pour the cooled custard into the pastry shells, filling each one almost full but leaving about a centimetre gap at the top. Bake for 25 minutes or until the custard has set. For authentic caramelised tops, place the tray under a hot grill for a few minutes to brown.

Eat immediately, or the same day, with a mug of tea or a tall glass of milky coffee, *um galao*, Portuguese-style.

Buns & Small Cakes

Avocado Chocolate Butterfly Cakes

Makes 12

40g unsalted butter, softened,
  plus extra for greasing
100g plain flour, plus extra for dusting
20g unsweetened cocoa powder
140g caster sugar
1½ tsp baking powder
A pinch of sea salt
120ml milk
1 egg, beaten
¼ tsp vanilla extract
Melted dark chocolate, for dipping
  (optional)

FOR THE AVOCADO BUTTERCREAM
1 ripe avocado, halved, stoned and peeled
200g icing sugar
Juice of ½ lemon

FOR CLASSIC VANILLA
BUTTERCREAM (IF YOU PREFER)
60g unsalted butter, softened
120g icing sugar
A few drops of vanilla extract

EQUIPMENT
12-hole muffin tray
Paper muffin cases (optional)

For an unusual 'buttercream', use avocado as an alternative. Avocado is actually a fruit, and in many parts of the world, such as Brazil and Indonesia, it is often used in sweet food such as milkshakes, ice creams and cakes. Some people think of it as a vegetable, only used in savoury dishes. Don't knock it till you try it, it works just as well in sweet dishes.

This recipe is my basic chocolate cake recipe, adapted from the Hummingbird Bakery cupcake recipe. It is also used for the BFG: My Black Forest Gateau recipe (see page 138) and the Paisley Cardamom Chocolate Cake recipe (see page 134). It is moist and works brilliantly.

Preheat the oven to 190°C (gas 5). Grease and lightly flour the holes of the muffin tray or line them with paper muffin cases.

In a stand mixer or by hand in a bowl, beat the butter until smooth, pale and fluffy, then add the flour, cocoa powder, caster sugar, baking powder and salt until well combined.

In a separate bowl, whisk the milk, egg and vanilla extract together. Pour half of the egg mixture into the butter mixture, beat together, then add the remaining egg mixture and beat together (remember to keep scraping the sides down).

Divide the mixture evenly into the prepared muffin tray holes. Bake for 15–20 minutes. They are done when a fine skewer inserted into the centre of the cakes comes out clean. Transfer to a wire rack to cool.

Make the buttercream. If you want to do an avocado buttercream, simply cream together all the ingredients until smooth and combined. For the classic vanilla buttercream, cream together the butter and icing sugar until pale and fluffy, then stir in the vanilla extract.

Once the cakes are completely cool, cut a horizontal slice from the top of each one and cut it in half for the 'wings'. Spread a spoonful of the buttercream on to the top of each cake, then place the 'wings' on top to resemble butterflies. You could also dip the wings into melted chocolate, then leave them to set before placing them on top, if you like.

Cupcakes Baked in a Cup

Makes 12

115g caster sugar
115g self-raising flour, plus extra for dusting
115g unsalted butter, softened, plus extra
    for greasing
2 eggs, beaten

FOR THE VANILLA
BUTTERCREAM ICING
300g icing sugar
150g unsalted butter, softened
A few drops of vanilla extract
A few drops of milk

Sprinkles, for decorating

EQUIPMENT
12 teacups (or bake them in batches)
Piping bag fitted with a wide star-shaped
    nozzle (optional)

Cupcakes are much derided these days, rather like 'yummy mummies'. Even feminist publications carry pieces that are prejudiced against yummy mummies, criticising them for their wide buggies that clog up chic coffee shops. It's true that some yummy mummies are ripe for parody, check out the @highgatemums feed on Twitter which has hilarious #firstworldproblems-type quotes from the upper-middle-class mums of Highgate in chic north London, such as 'a friend was working at school, and asked a 4-year-old boy what his favourite colour was. He immediately replied "champagne".' But do we want to return to the days when stay-at-home mothers kept quiet, were frumpy and stayed indoors?

The original cupcakes were so named because they were baked in teacups (in a range cooker, as it cooled off). I figured I'd try the same thing. After all, porcelain and pottery are baked in a kiln at a very high temperature so an oven should be safe.

It means less washing up and they look cute! Just like yummy mummies, in fact...

Preheat the oven to 150°C (gas 2). Grease the insides of your teacups using butter (or a vegetable oil spray). You could also put a sprinkling of flour inside. Line a baking sheet with a damp tea towel (an extra precaution to avoid cracking).

Tip all the cake ingredients into a bowl and mix together until smooth. Spoon the mixture into your prepared teacups, then place the teacups on the baking sheet. Bake for about 15 minutes or until a skewer inserted into the centre of a cake comes out clean. Leave the cups to cool on the baking sheet.

For the buttercream, in a bowl, mix together the icing sugar, butter, vanilla extract and a little milk until the buttercream binds, is light and fluffy and is not too sloppy. Spread with a palette knife or pipe on to your cakes, add sprinkles and enjoy with a nice cup of tea.

Ginger Blondies

Makes 12 small blondies

120g unsalted butter, cubed,
   plus extra for greasing
250g soft light brown sugar
1 large egg, beaten
125g plain flour, plus extra for dusting
1 tsp vanilla salt, or ½ tsp sea salt
   and ½ tsp vanilla paste
2.5cm piece of fresh root ginger, peeled
   and finely grated
250g good-quality white chocolate, finely
   chopped, plus extra melted for drizzling
50g skinned hazelnuts or macadamia nuts,
   roughly chopped

EQUIPMENT
Shallow 20cm square cake tin
Fine grater such as a Microplane
   (for grating the fresh ginger)

Blondies have more fun! This recipe makes lovely squidgy blond–ies with the wonderful flavour of fresh ginger, which undercuts the very sweet white chocolate.

Preheat the oven to 180°C (gas 4). Grease the cake tin and dust with flour, tapping out any excess.

Melt the butter in a bowl in the microwave (on full power), or carefully in a small pan over a low heat. Pour into a large bowl and mix with the sugar. Add the egg and beat together until smooth, then fold in the flour and salt. Mix in the grated ginger and taste, adding a little more ginger if you'd like a stronger ginger taste.

Stir in the chopped chocolate and nuts, then pour into the pre-pared tin. Tap the tin a couple of times to get rid of any big bubbles.

Bake for 20–35 minutes, testing for readiness at 20 minutes. Err on the side of undercooked as the blondies solidify when they cool. You want stickiness!

Remove from the oven and leave to cool completely in the tin. Once cool, drizzle some melted white chocolate over the cake and leave it to set, before cutting into squares.

Spelt Cinnamon Buns (*Kanelbullar*)

Makes 35–37

500g plain flour, plus extra for dusting
350g spelt flour
50g fresh yeast, crumbled
125g cane sugar
1 heaped tsp sea salt
2 tsp cardamom seeds, ground
500ml milk, at room temperature
180g unsalted butter, cubed
   (at room temperature)
Milk or 1 beaten egg, to glaze
Cane sugar (I used Steenbergs Vanilla
   Sugar – see page 250 for stockists) or
   soft light brown sugar, for sprinkling

FOR THE FILLING
100g salted butter, softened
50g cane sugar
1 tbsp ground cinnamon
1½ tsp water

Icing sugar (or cinnamon sugar),
   for dusting (optional)

EQUIPMENT
2 rectangular baking/cake tins
   (each about 34 x 28cm)

In Kastellgatan Street in Gothenburg live the strongest girls in Sweden. Fanny, Lizette and Sabina have shapely, muscly arms and broad shoulders; every day they work from the middle of the night, and then through the whole day, and their husbands never see them. (But their husbands still love them for they smell of yeast, cinnamon, sweat and sugar.) These ladies dress like pirates in striped T-shirts, bandanas and rolled-up trousers; they wear no make-up, bar the fine white flour that dusts their pale complexions. Fanny is their leader: this is her recipe. She owns the sourdough bakery Alvar and Ivar, in Gothenburg.

Line your baking tins with parchment paper or silicone mats.

Put the two flours, yeast, sugar, salt, ground cardamom and milk in a bowl, add the butter and mix with a wooden spoon or in a stand mixer for 5 minutes to make a dough. It should be smooth and a bit shiny. Cover and leave to rest in a warm place for 20 minutes, then tip on to a lightly floured work surface and divide it into two equal pieces. Shape each piece into a round loaf and put them in the fridge for 1 hour to rest.

Meanwhile, for the filling, mix together the butter, sugar, cinnamon and water to make a paste.

Take one piece of chilled dough, tip it on to a well-floured work surface and roll it out to a rectangle, approximately 20 x 30cm in size and 3mm thick. Gently spread half of the filling paste all over the dough using a palette knife or dough scraper.

Starting at the top of the short edge, carefully fold the edge of the dough and start rolling it towards you. You want a thinnish roll so that you get more filling in your bun. When you have a nice roll, cut it into 2.5cm slices and place upright in a prepared baking tin, then cover the tin with a clean tea towel.

Repeat with the second loaf of dough. Leave both tins to rise somewhere warm until the buns have doubled in size.

Preheat the oven to 240°C (gas 9).

Brush the buns with milk or beaten egg to glaze, sprinkle with sugar and bake for around 5 minutes or until golden brown. Transfer to a wire rack to cool. Serve warm or cold, pulled apart into separate buns, and dusted with icing sugar, if you like.

Doughnuts

Makes 20

500g strong white bread flour,
    plus extra for dusting
7g sachet fast-action dried yeast
½ tsp sea salt
275g caster sugar
250ml milk
30g unsalted butter
2 eggs, beaten
About 250g fruit curd
    (Lemon Curd, see page 122
    Passion Fruit Curd, see page 41
    or Sweet/Sour Gooseberry Curd,
    see page 42)
Vegetable oil, for deep-frying

EQUIPMENT
5cm round cutter
2cm round cutter
Piping bag fitted with a small plain nozzle

I'm not a doughnut lover, unless I make my own, when I can eat them hot and oozing, straight out of the fryer. You could try dusting them with different flavoured sugars like lavender- or cinnamon-infused sugars (see page 232).

Put the flour, yeast, salt and 75g of the sugar into a bowl.

Warm the milk and butter in a small pan over a medium heat, taking it off the heat when the butter starts to melt. Beat the eggs into the warmed mixture and then pour this into your bowl of dry ingredients. Using your hands, knead the dough until it is smooth – this will take about 5 minutes.

Pat the dough into a round ball and place it in a greased bowl. Leave to rise until doubled in size, around 1–2 hours.

Knock back the dough and knead until smooth, then cover the bowl with cling film and leave it in the fridge to rise for up to 12 hours.

Line 2 baking sheets with parchment paper or silicone mats.

Roll out the risen dough on a lightly floured work surface to 2–3cm thickness. Cut out 5cm rounds and then make 2cm holes in the middle of the rounds. They might look smaller than shop-bought doughnuts but they expand in the fryer.

Place the doughnuts at least 2cm apart on the baking sheets and cover with cling film. Leave them to prove until doubled in size.

If you have a deep-fat fryer, preheat it to 180°C. If not, use a deep pan or wok, filling it with a good few centimetres of clean vegetable oil. The oil is hot enough when a cube of bread turns golden within 15 seconds.

Carefully drop the doughnuts into the oil, without splashing, frying a batch at a time, until golden brown. They fry really quickly so do keep an eye on them. Once golden, use a slotted spoon to scoop them out of the oil and transfer to kitchen paper. Repeat until all the doughnuts are cooked.

Coat the warm doughnuts with the remaining caster sugar, then cut a small hole in the side of each doughnut, driving it either side of the hole in the middle. Fill the piping bag with the fruit curd and poke the tip of the nozzle into each doughnut. Fill with delicious sweet curd.

Best eaten on the day with a cup of tea.

Big Cakes

I like a variety of shapes of cake at a tea party: some large cakes, cut into slices, and some smaller cakes, just enough for one person. Big cakes last longer and can be used for celebrations such as birthdays.

Cherokee Blueberry Honey Cake

Serves 8–10

120g unsalted butter, plus extra for greasing
85g light muscovado sugar
170g honey (runny or thick, doesn't matter)
2 eggs, beaten
200g self-raising flour, plus 1 tbsp,
  plus extra for dusting
½ tsp sea salt
300g fresh blueberries
Icing sugar, for dusting

EQUIPMENT
2kg bundt tin

Don't make the mistake I once made in an American café and order a 'dingleberry' pie.

Here is the recipe for a Cherokee Blueberry Honey Cake (sounds like the name of a pop star's progeny). It is beautifully moist and not too sweet. The original recipe used huckleberries*, but those being thin on the ground in north–west London, I replaced them with blueberries. I was told by a guest that huckleberries aren't actually very nice!

I made this in a 2kg bundt tin, but you can also halve the recipe and make it in a 1kg loaf tin. When using bundt tins, make sure the cake is completely cool before turning it out.

Preheat the oven to 180°C (gas 4). Grease the bundt tin and dust with flour, tapping out any excess.

Gently heat the butter, muscovado sugar and honey together in a pan over a low heat until combined and smooth. Remove from the heat. Add the eggs and sift in the 200g flour and the salt. Mix well.

Dust the fresh blueberries with the extra tablespoon of flour.

I tip some of the blueberries into the prepared tin, then half the cake mixture, the rest of the blueberries, then the last of the cake mixture, and bake it for 1 hour. Honey cakes are notoriously unstable, so try not to open the oven door until the mixture is set, say after 40 minutes. It's done when a fine skewer inserted into the centre of the cake comes out clean.

Leave the cake to cool completely in the tin, then turn out and dust with icing sugar to serve.

Lemon Polenta Cake

Serves 15–20

175g finely ground polenta
55g plain flour
1 tsp baking powder
¼ tsp sea salt
5 tbsp creamy natural yoghurt
5 tbsp walnut or sunflower oil
Finely grated zest and juice of 2 plump
   lemons
2 tbsp runny honey
½ tsp glycerine
2 eggs plus 2 egg whites
200g caster sugar
100g demerara sugar
Butter, for greasing

FOR THE SUGAR SYRUP
150ml water
150g demerara sugar
Finely grated zest and juice of 1 lemon
4 tbsp thick honey
1 tsp finely chopped fresh rosemary

EQUIPMENT
1kg loaf tin
Sugar thermometer

This is a guest recipe from La Sagra secret tearoom. Angie started La Sagra in her living room in Putney, west London (see page 248), after being inspired by my *Supper Club* book. She bakes English specialities, but she also makes a few Italian-style cakes, having spent many years living in Italy. This delicious cake has a lot of ingredients to prepare, but mixing it together is very quick and simple and, more importantly, it tastes wonderful. If you have a 'gluten-free' guest, swap the flour for ground almonds.

Preheat the oven to 180°C (gas 4). Grease the loaf tin.

Sift the polenta, flour, baking powder and salt into a bowl.

In a separate bowl or jug, mix together the yoghurt, oil, lemon zest and juice, honey and glycerine.

In another large bowl, beat together the whole eggs, the egg whites and both sugars until creamy, then beat in the yoghurt mixture and fold in the dry ingredients until just combined.

Pour the mixture into the prepared tin and bake for 45–50 minutes or until springy to the touch. Leave the cake to cool completely in the tin.

To make the sugar syrup, boil the water, sugar, lemon zest and juice, honey and rosemary together in a pan over a medium-high heat until the temperature reaches 100°C (or simmer for approximately 10 minutes). You want the mixture to reach the consistency of runny honey. Remove from the heat.

Pour the syrup generously over the cooled cake. Be brave and drown it in syrup – it will soak through the sponge, making an indulgent, delicious and moist cake. Leave the cake for at least a couple of hours or even a day before you turn it out (it will absorb more of the syrup), and then serve it.

Mars Bar Cheesecake

Serves 8-10

200g digestive biscuits
190g unsalted butter, softened
2 tbsp caster sugar
350ml crème fraîche
80g milk chocolate, chopped
5 platinum gelatine leaves (see page 156)
300g ricotta
200g plain fromage frais
100g icing sugar
1 Mars bar (51g), diced into 1cm squares

EQUIPMENT
Deep 20cm round loose-based cake tin

I found this recipe on the back of a French magazine when I was living in Provence. I've rarely seen Mars bars for sale in France, so I waited till I was back in the UK to make it. It's actually not as sweet as it sounds, but lovely and gooey.

Line the cake tin with cling film.

Crush the biscuits and combine with 150g of the butter, then press the mixture firmly into the base of the prepared cake tin and chill in the fridge while you make the filling.

Mix the caster sugar, the remaining 40g butter and 4 tablespoons of the crème fraîche in a small pan over a low heat. Heat gently, while whisking, until it forms a thick cream. Remove from the heat and set aside.

In another pan, mix together the chocolate and 4 tablespoons of the remaining crème fraîche. Heat gently, whisking. When the chocolate is melted, remove from the heat and set aside.

Soak the gelatine leaves in cold water for 10 minutes. Squeeze out the water, then put the gelatine in a bowl and microwave (on full power) for 10 seconds or until the gelatine is dissolved. (Alternatively, you could use a bain-marie to do this – see page 69.) Remove from the heat and leave to cool.

In a bowl, whisk together the ricotta, fromage frais and icing sugar. Add the remaining crème fraîche and the dissolved gelatine, followed by the Mars bar pieces.

Put half the cheesecake mixture on to the biscuit base. Smooth it over, then add a thin layer of half the cream topping and a thin layer of half the chocolate topping. Use a fork to swirl the two toppings together to create a marbled pattern.

Add the rest of the cheesecake mixture and smooth it over, then the remaining chocolate topping and smooth it over in a thin layer. Finally, drizzle the remaining cream topping in thin parallel lines across the top of the cheesecake and then use the edge of a fork or knife to mark patterns on top.

Chill for at least a couple of hours to set, but make sure you take it out of the fridge an hour or so before serving so that the flavours can come to the fore.

Baked New York Cheesecake

Serves 16

FOR THE BASE
400g Nice biscuits
160g unsalted butter, melted

FOR THE FILLING
3 eggs, separated
750g quark
225g cream cheese or crème fraîche
200g caster sugar
4 tbsp neutral cooking oil, such as
    sunflower oil, plus extra for greasing
1 vanilla pod, split in half lengthways and
    seeds scraped out, or 1 tsp vanilla extract
Finely grated zest of 1 lemon
20g cornflour

TO FINISH AND DECORATE
100g demerara sugar
Fresh berries, to top
    (I used 500g blackberries)

EQUIPMENT
23cm springform cake tin

I've made a few cheesecakes over the years, but this is a nice recipe from my extremely hard-working chef friend James Benson. Using quark, it has a lovely fudgy, stick-to-the-roof-of-your-mouth texture while being lighter than some versions.

Grease the cake tin with sunflower oil.

For the base, whizz the Nice biscuits in a food processor until they resemble fine breadcrumbs. Add the melted butter and mix through until well combined.

Spread the biscuit mix over the base and about 5 cms up the sides of the tin. It's important not to have it too thick where the sides meet the base, so press it into the corners evenly so that's it's the same thickness all over.

Chill the base in the fridge for at least 30 minutes, or even overnight if you want to make the cheesecake the next day.

Preheat the oven to 170°C (gas 3).

For the filling, place all the filling ingredients, apart from the egg whites, in a large mixing bowl and mix together with a whisk until smooth – this may also be done in a stand mixer on its lowest setting. In another mixing bowl, whisk the egg whites until stiff. Now, fold the egg whites into the cheesecake mix until combined.

Remove the cheesecake base from the fridge. Shake out any loose biscuit crumbs, which would spoil the appearance of the finished cheesecake. Place the base (still in the tin) on a baking sheet and then pour in the filling.

Bake in the bottom half of the oven for 50–60 minutes. Do not open the oven door until the last 10 minutes. The cheesecake will rise slightly. It is done when you wobble it on the baking sheet and it barely moves. It continues cooking after it is taken out of the oven and cools down. If it is left in the oven too long, it will crack as it cools down.

When the cheesecake is done, turn off the oven, open the door and allow the cheesecake to come to room temperature in the oven. Remove and refrigerate until ready to serve.

For a million-dollar finish, just before serving, remove the cheesecake from the tin, sprinkle the top with the demerara sugar and caramelise it either under a hot grill or with a blowtorch for a crème brûlée-style topping. Then, top with fresh berries.

Elderflower Cheesecakes

Serves 6

150g digestive biscuits, crushed
75g salted butter, melted
100g caster sugar
225ml whipping cream
225g cream cheese
1 vanilla pod, cut in half lengthways
  and seeds scraped out, or a few drops of vanilla extract
50ml elderflower cordial
Small sprigs of fresh elderflowers,
  to decorate (optional)

EQUIPMENT
6 glass ramekins (each about 150ml)

Elderflower is in season in June. It's one of the easier edible flowers to forage as it grows like a weed in London and other cities in the UK and is prolific further afield in the countryside too. It has a heady floral flavour. These aren't big cakes, but they're big on flavour, so we'll allow them here.

In a bowl, mix together the crushed biscuits and melted butter. Press this mixture evenly into the bottoms of the ramekins.

Put the sugar into a small pan and heat over a medium heat until it melts. Remove from the heat and leave to cool.

In a separate bowl, whip the cream to form soft peaks. In another bowl, beat together the cream cheese, vanilla seeds or extract, cooled sugar syrup and the elderflower cordial. Fold in the whipped cream.

Spoon the mixture into the ramekins, dividing evenly, and then decorate with sprigs of elderflowers, if you like. Chill in the fridge for a couple of hours or so before serving.

Lemon, Almond and Pistachio Cake with Lemon Cream Frosting

Serves 8-10

250g unsalted butter, softened, plus extra
    for greasing
250g caster sugar
3 large eggs
100g shelled pistachios, crushed or ground
100g ground almonds
60g plain flour
1 tsp baking powder
Finely grated zest and juice of 1 large lemon
1 tsp vanilla extract

FOR THE LEMON CURD
(MAKES MORE THAN YOU NEED)
Finely grated zest and juice of 3 large lemons
175g golden caster sugar
100g unsalted butter, cubed
2 large eggs, beaten, plus 1 egg yolk, beaten

FOR THE FROSTING
AND DECORATION
300ml double cream
3 tbsp lemon curd (from recipe above)
180g nibbed pistachios
Lemon zest curls

EQUIPMENT
23cm springform cake tin
1 x 450g sterilised jam jar (see page 41)

Gwyneth Brock runs monthly vintage afternoon teas from her 18th-century farmhouse in Bowdon, near Manchester (see page 249). She says, 'It's two days' work for a tea party for twenty, and that's now that I've got it down to a tee [but] the table groans with cake... we wear vintage pinnies [and] I make a bit of an effort with a frock.'

Preheat the oven to 180°C (gas 4). Grease and line the cake tin with parchment paper.

Cream the butter and sugar together until pale and fluffy. Add the eggs, one at a time, beating well after each addition. Fold in all the remaining cake ingredients and then pour the mixture into the prepared cake tin.

Bake for around 1 hour, covering the cake with foil at 40 minutes to prevent burning. Leave to cool in the tin for 10 minutes, then unclip the sides of the tin and slide the cake on to a wire rack to cool completely.

Meanwhile, make the lemon curd for the frosting. Put the lemon zest and juice, sugar and butter in a heatproof bowl set over a pan of simmering water (making sure the bowl doesn't touch the simmering water underneath), and stir with a whisk until the butter has melted. Stir in the eggs and egg yolk and heat gently, stirring constantly, until the curd thickens. Do not allow it to boil or it will curdle. Remove from the heat. While the curd is still hot, pour it into the sterilised jar, cover, seal and label. Leave to cool, then store in the fridge and use within 2 weeks.

For the frosting and decoration, whip the cream in a bowl with 3 tablespoons of the cold lemon curd to form firmish peaks, and then smooth it over the top of the cool cake using a palette knife. Sprinkle with the nibbed pistachios and lemon zest curls.

Passion Fruit Cloud Cake

Serves 8–10

200g digestive biscuits, finely crushed
90g unsalted or salted butter, melted,
   plus extra for greasing
600ml double cream
3 large egg whites
450g caster sugar
¼ tsp cream of tartar, sifted
200ml passion fruit juice
Seeds and juice of 6 passion fruit
White-chocolate-dipped Physalis
   (see page 152), to decorate (optional)

EQUIPMENT
23cm springform cake tin

Passion fruits are one of my favourites; I love sour foods. Passion fruits are ready to be eaten when their skins are slightly wrinkly. A smooth passion fruit is under-ripe. Choose heavy fruit, as these will contain the most pulp.

This is a fluffy, luxurious frozen dessert that's easy to make and designed to be eaten as soon as it is removed from the freezer. It takes very little time to prepare, then just bung it in the freezer for 4 hours. Job done.

Grease the cake tin, then line the base with a circle of parchment paper.

Mix together the biscuit crumbs and melted butter and then press the mixture evenly into the base of the prepared tin. Chill in the fridge or freezer while you prepare the topping.

Whip the cream in a bowl to soft peaks and then chill.

In a clean, grease-free bowl, whisk together the egg whites, 250g of the sugar and the cream of tartar on high speed (using an electric hand-held whisk or stand mixer) for 5–6 minutes or until the mixture is very thick and fluffy and the sugar has dissolved into the mixture. Test by rubbing a little of the mixture between your fingers, it should not feel gritty. Carefully fold the whipped cream into the meringue, then gently fold in the passion fruit juice until completely incorporated.

Spoon the mixture over the chilled biscuit base and smooth the top. Cover with cling film or a sheet of parchment paper, place in the freezer and freeze for at least 4 hours.

Meanwhile, put the passion fruit seeds and juice in a pan with the remaining sugar and simmer, stirring occasionally, until the sugar has dissolved and it starts to form a thick syrup. Remove from the heat and leave to cool.

Just before serving, remove the Cloud Cake from the freezer, remove it from the tin, place on a serving plate and then spoon the passion fruit topping over the top. You can also add another wonderfully sweet/sour fruit to decorate, if you like... physalis dipped in white chocolate.

Ice Cream Cakes

Children's tea parties have jelly and ice cream as standard issue. An adult tea party can bestow similar pleasures but with a little more sophistication and, according to an impromptu Twitter poll that I held while writing this, the addition of alcohol. Here are some ideas.

Sour Cherry and Meringue Alaskan Arctic Roll

Serves 15

FOR THE SOUR CHERRY
ICE CREAM
150g caster sugar
20g cornflour
A small pinch of sea salt
200ml milk
400ml soured cream
1 jar (280g) sour cherry jam
    (often you can get this in Middle
    Eastern or Polish shops)

FOR THE SWISS ROLL SPONGE
4 large eggs
100g caster sugar
1 tsp vanilla extract
100g plain flour, sifted

FOR THE CHERRY JAM LAYER
150g sour cherries, stoned
    (or normal cherries, stoned, with 1½ tsp
    citric acid added)
40g caster sugar
2 tbsp kirsch

FOR THE SWISS MERINGUE
400g golden caster sugar
50ml water
6 egg whites

Fresh cherries, to serve

EQUIPMENT
Ice cream maker

The sour cherry ice cream in this recipe is from Swedish supper club host and chef, the beautiful Linn Soderstrom. She's a professional chef but also runs a monthly supper club at her house in Stockholm (see page 249). 'My parents have three cherry trees and their freezer is full of the sour and sweet berries. This is my father's favourite dessert and I make it every time I visit my parents' house.'

Sour cherries are common in Sweden, but it's difficult to find sour cherries in the UK so use sour cherry jam, unless you happen to know someone with a sour cherry tree! You are looking for the Morello, Early Richmond or Montmorency varieties. My 'hack' is to add a little citric acid to the cherry jam filling to get that sour vibe. I've also found frozen Iranian sour cherries in Middle Eastern shops; they taste amazing but make sure you pit them.

It's important to make a light sponge, so pay attention to getting as much air into your mixture as possible. A simpler version would be without the meringue - i.e. arctic roll, one of my favourite school dinners - but with the meringue added to the arctic roll on the outside in this recipe, it defies belief!

First, make the sour cherry ice cream. Put the sugar, cornflour and salt, plus 2 tablespoons of the milk, in a small pan over a low heat. Whisk the mixture together as you warm it, then once it's warm, add the rest of the milk. Continue to whisk until it thickens, making sure you scrape the sides and bottom of the pan to prevent scorching. The mixture will become translucent, meaning that the cornflour has been cooked through properly.

Remove from the heat and gradually whisk together the hot mixture with the soured cream, then stir in the sour cherry jam. Set aside to cool, then churn and freeze in your ice cream maker until softly set. If you don't have an ice cream maker, then pour the mixture into a shallow plastic sealable container. Place in the freezer and every 30 minutes or so, whisk the ice cream mixture vigorously in the container to prevent any hard crystals forming. The ice cream will take 2–3 hours to become softly set, so you'll need to whisk it 4–6 times.

Preheat the oven to 180°C (gas 4). Line a baking sheet with parchment paper or a silicone mat.

Whisk the eggs in a bowl with an electric hand-held whisk, then gradually add the sugar until the mixture is fluffy and white and has doubled in volume, almost meringue-like. Fold in the vanilla extract and then the flour.

Carefully, using a palette knife, spread the mixture into an even rectangle (about 30 x 20cm) on the prepared baking sheet, rather like making a Swiss roll.

Bake for 12 minutes or until springy to the touch, but you must keep an eye on it, as it cooks fast! Remove from the oven, cover the sponge with a damp tea towel to stop it drying out, and leave it to cool completely (with the tea towel cover on until completely cold).

Meanwhile, make the cherry jam layer by heating the cherries, citric acid if using, sugar and kirsch together in a pan over a medium heat, until thick and jammy, stirring occasionally. Remove from the heat and leave to cool completely.

Invert the cooled sponge on to a clean sheet of parchment paper. Remove the lining paper, trim off any burnt edges and carefully spread the cherry jam mixture over the sponge. Then, using a palette knife and working quickly, spread the softly set ice cream over the jam layer, about 2–3cm thick.

Fold over the first 2mm of the long side of the sponge and, using the paper to help you, roll up the sponge, making sure the seam is at the bottom. Discard the paper, cover the arctic roll with cling film and freeze for 2 hours.

Meanwhile, make the Swiss meringue. Put the sugar and water into a heavy-based pan. Bring to the boil over a medium-high heat, shaking the pan to move the sugar around so it dissolves, then bubble until golden and thickened (this takes about 10 minutes). Make sure it doesn't crystallise by brushing the sides of the pan with a heatproof pastry brush dipped in water. Once it is ready, remove from the heat.

Place the egg whites in the bowl of a stand mixer and begin to whisk, gradually adding the hot sugar syrup, then whisk continuously until the mixture has cooled, approximately 20 minutes.

Meanwhile, preheat the oven to 220°C (gas 7). Line a baking sheet with parchment paper or a silicone mat.

Take the arctic roll out of the freezer, remove the cling film and trim the ends of the roll to neaten it. Place it on the prepared baking sheet and liberally spread the meringue over the sponge with a palette knife, shaping it into peaks. Place the fresh cherries with stems along the top of the cake.

Bake for 10 minutes, until the peaks of the meringue are golden. Alternatively, instead of baking it, use a blowtorch to 'cook' the meringue until golden all over.

Serve immediately, or freeze. What is great with this dessert is that the Swiss meringue does not disintegrate in the freezer. Yes, you can serve it as a frozen dessert. It keeps for up to 2 weeks in the freezer.

Raspberry and Toblerone Swiss Bombe

Serves 8–10

10 large eggs, separated
350g caster sugar
350g good-quality dark chocolate,
   broken into pieces
150ml water

FOR THE RASPBERRY
BUTTERCREAM FILLING
500g fresh raspberries
200g unsalted butter, softened
500g icing sugar
Juice of ½ lemon
1 tsp vanilla extract
A pinch of sea salt
A little milk (optional)

FOR THE ICE CREAM
2 litres of your favourite vanilla
   or raspberry ripple ice cream
400g white, milk or dark chocolate
   Toblerone bars, chopped into
   small pieces

EQUIPMENT
Two 28 x 35 x 2cm shallow baking/cake tins
2-litre large metal or Pyrex bowl

The Swiss are famously neutral politically; this bombe with an 'e' is an ice cream cake that is easier to make than it looks.

First, make the raspberry buttercream. Put 350g of the raspberries in a pan over a medium heat and stir frequently until the raspberries are broken down into a sauce. Remove from the heat and strain, keeping back a tablespoon of the pulp for the buttercream icing (it adds a little grit). Return the sauce to the pan and simmer for about 10 minutes, until thick. Remove from the heat and set aside to cool completely.

Using a stand mixer with a paddle attachment on medium-high speed, or in a bowl using a wooden spoon, cream the butter for about 2 minutes, until lightened in colour and a bit fluffy. Add 400g of the icing sugar, then the cooled raspberry sauce, the reserved tablespoon of the pulp, the lemon juice, vanilla extract and salt. Mix until smooth, then add the remaining icing sugar. If it's too stiff, add a little milk to loosen it up. Cover and chill until needed.

Preheat the oven to 180°C (gas 4). Line the baking tins with parchment paper or silicone mats.

Now, make the Swiss roll sponges. In a large bowl, whisk the egg yolks and sugar together until the mixture is pale and falls in a ribbon from the whisk. You will have to do this with a stand mixer or an electric hand-held whisk, rather than by hand, unless you have biceps like Popeye. Set aside.

Heat the chocolate and water together in a bowl in the microwave (on full power) in 30-second bursts until the chocolate has melted, or in a bain-marie (see page 69), making sure the bowl doesn't touch the simmering water underneath. Add the melted chocolate mix to the egg yolk mix, combining lightly.

In a separate bowl, whisk the egg whites to stiff peaks. Fold, don't stir, the chocolate mix into the egg whites, then pour the cake mix into your prepared baking tins, tilting the tins backwards and forwards, making sure the cake mix evenly covers the whole surface of the parchment paper/silicone mat in the tins. You are aiming for thin and even sponges, that can be rolled up into Swiss rolls.

Bake for 12–15 minutes or until springy to the touch. Remove from the oven and then leave to cool for 5 minutes before turning out each sponge on to a clean sheet of parchment paper. Roll up each one from the long side with the paper inside. Cover with damp tea towels until ready to use. This is to stop the sponges drying out – you are trying to prevent your soft Swiss rolls from cracking when you fill and roll them. They may still crack and that's fine, but try to avoid it if possible.

Once the sponge cakes are cool, unroll each one, then using a spatula, spread the raspberry buttercream all over the sponges. Roll up the sponges again tightly, then cover with cling film and chill in the fridge for at least 2 hours.

For the ice cream, allow the ice cream to soften slightly by removing it from the freezer and putting it in the fridge, while you do the next step.

Line the large metal or Pyrex bowl with cling film. Take the sponge rolls out of the fridge and cut them into 2cm slices. Place the coiled rounds of Swiss roll closely all over the inside of the prepared bowl (right up to the rim), leaving enough slices to cover the top of the bombe later.

Now your ice cream should be soft enough to work with (but still frozen), so remove it from the fridge and then, working quickly, mix the Toblerone pieces into the ice cream. Tip it into the cake-lined bowl, filling the bowl to the rim, then cover the top with the remaining slices of Swiss roll. Cover with cling film and place in the freezer for 2 hours or until firm.

When you want to serve your bombe, pull away the cling film from the top of the bowl and invert the cake on to a serving plate. Remove the bowl and peel off the rest of the cling film. Place the rest of the reserved raspberries around the base. Serve in 5 minutes or so.

Spectacular
Centrepieces

Every afternoon tea needs a beautifully presented knock-out dish that dominates the table. The French call it a *pièce montée*. This is when you can go mad with ornate large dishes or cake stands. A centrepiece dish gives your afternoon tea wow factor. Here are some simpler large cakes and a few maximalist ideas and recipes.

Paisley Cardamom Chocolate Cake

Serves 8–10

80g unsalted butter, softened,
  plus extra for greasing
200g plain flour, plus extra for dusting
40g unsweetened cocoa powder
280g caster sugar
3 tsp baking powder
2 pinches of sea salt
240ml milk
2 eggs
2 tsp vanilla extract

FOR THE CHOCOLATE LACE
100g easy-melt dark chocolate
  (I used Squires Kitchen– see stockists
  on page 250), broken into pieces

FOR THE CARDAMOM
BUTTERCREAM
250g unsalted butter, softened
500g icing sugar
2 tsp cardamom seeds, ground
50ml milk or single cream

100g nibbed pistachios, to decorate
  (see stockists on page 250)

EQUIPMENT
2 x 20cm sandwich tins
Piping bag fitted with small round nozzle
  or small tip cut from bag
Silicone (or parchment) paper

This recipe uses a classic chocolate cake sponge, but I add exoti-cism with a cardamom buttercream, chocolate 'lace' and a sprin-kling of grass–green pistachios.

Nibbed pistachios are made by hand in Iran. You can get them from Middle Eastern shops and Persepolis, a marvellous Alad-din's cave of a shop in Peckham, London, run by my friend and fellow cookbook author, Sally Butcher. (She wrote *Veggiestan* and *Snackistan*, both of which I recommend.)

Chocolate lace is easier to make than it looks, depending on your design. I based mine on paisley, which you often find on Indian shawls. The key thing is to make sure all the chocolate joins up. This is quite delicate, so make spares. Buy an easy–melt dark chocolate coating that is already tempered and melt it in a bain–marie (see page 69), making sure the bowl doesn't touch the simmering water underneath, or melt it briefly in a bowl in the microwave (on full power) in 30–second bursts. You can then put it into a piping bag.

I printed a paisley design I found on the internet and taped the design to the table with some silicone (or parchment) paper on top. I then cut a very small tip from my piping bag and piped the chocolate on to the design, linking up the little circles, then let it dry and carefully peeled it off the paper.

Preheat the oven to 170°C (gas 3). Grease and flour the tins, or grease and base-line them with parchment paper. Have your chocolate de-sign and silicone (or parchment) paper ready.

In a stand mixer or by hand in a bowl, beat the butter until smooth, pale and fluffy, then mix in the flour, cocoa powder, sugar, baking powder and salt until well combined.

In a separate bowl, whisk together the milk, eggs and vanilla extract. Pour half of the egg mixture into the butter mixture, beat together until combined, then add the remaining egg mixture and beat together (don't overbeat). Keep scraping down the sides so that all the ingredients are incorporated. Tip half of the mixture into each prepared tin and smooth the tops.

Bake for 20–25 minutes or until a skewer inserted into the centre comes out clean. Turn out, invert and leave to cool on a wire rack.

While the cake is baking, melt the chocolate for the chocolate lace and fill your piping bag. Pipe out the design on the silicone (or parchment) paper (see recipe introduction) and transfer the chocolate lace to the fridge or set aside to cool. The chocolate lace will start to curl off the paper, so carefully prise them all off.

Make the cardamom buttercream by beating the butter in a bowl until fluffy, then add the icing sugar, ground cardamom and milk or cream. Beat until well combined.

Once the cakes are cool, slather a layer of buttercream over one sponge layer, sandwich together with the second sponge layer and then apply a thin 'crumb crust' of buttercream around the sides and over the top of the cake. Then, using a palette knife, add the final layer of buttercream to cover the cake.

Apply the chocolate paisley designs or whichever design you have decided upon, by pressing them gently around the sides of the cake while the buttercream is still tacky. Scatter the nibbed pistachios over the top of the cake.

Lovely with some Indian tea such as Darjeeling.

Napoleon Cake

Serves 8–10

3 packs (320g each) all-butter
ready-rolled puff pastry sheets, chilled
(sheets make it easier and quicker)
250g salted butter, softened
400g tin condensed milk (shop-bought
or home-made – see page 44)
250g skinned/blanched hazelnuts,
left whole
Plain flour, for dusting

EQUIPMENT
20cm cake tin or plate
(to use as a template)

This is a bastardised form of a famous cake beloved by the Russians. You need an awful lot of condensed milk for this moreish and diabetic-coma-inducing speciality. You can buy it in cans or make your own, which is easier than you think and healthier, and you won't be supporting a multinational in the process.

For this recipe, you need to make a millefeuille pastry, which is French for 'a thousand leaves'. One Lincolnshire chef said to me 'Oh, you mean milly filly pastry!', which I thought was cute. You could make your own puff pastry but here I suggest you buy good-quality all-butter puff pastry.

Preheat the oven to 200°C (gas 6). Line 2 or 3 baking sheets with parchment paper or silicone mats.

Prepare a clean work surface and have a little bit of flour ready for dusting. Take one sheet of pastry, flatten it first with your hands, then roll it out carefully with a rolling pin to about 3mm thickness and cut out two circles (each about 20cm in diameter). Using your rolling pin, lift each circle and carefully place it on to a prepared baking sheet. Prick with a fork in several places to stop bubbles forming while baking, or place another baking sheet on top for the first few minutes of baking to flatten each one down.

Repeat with the remaining pastry sheets (cutting 2 circles of pastry from each sheet). You want 6 pastry circles in total. You'll need to bake the circles in several batches (make sure you keep the unbaked pastry chilled).

Bake 2 or 3 circles at a time for about 15 minutes or until they are lightly browned. Remove from the oven and leave to cool completely on the baking sheets.

While the pastry is cooking, beat together the butter and condensed milk to form a cream. Set aside at room temperature.

Once the pastry is cool, start layering your Napoleon. Place one pastry circle on a serving plate or board, spread some of the cream over it, then put another pastry circle on top, and so on, finishing with a final layer of cream. Decorate the top of the cake with the hazelnuts. Leave to stand at room temperature for 2–3 hours (to allow the cream to soak into the pastry layers), then transfer to the fridge overnight or even for the whole day to set.

The BFG: My Black Forest Gateau

Serves 8–10

80g unsalted butter, softened, plus extra
    for greasing
200g plain flour, plus extra for dusting
40g unsweetened cocoa powder
280g caster sugar
3 tsp baking powder
2 pinches of sea salt
240ml milk
2 eggs
2 tsp vanilla extract
1 jar (390g) black cherries in kirsch,
    drained, cherries and kirsch retained
    separately
600ml double cream
250g fresh cherries
2 tbsp icing sugar

EQUIPMENT
2 x 20cm sandwich tins

For a winter tea party I wanted to make something that suggested snow ploughing between pine trees, deep evergreen forests and beautiful hoar frosts. As a child I loved the food we had when we went skiing: *glühwein*, frankfurters, sauerkraut and mash with yellow Austrian mustard, *raclette*, cheese fondue and hot, frothy chocolate drinks. And, of course, Black Forest Gateau.

There is something shiny and pornographic about the cherry. This leads me inevitably to baking a Black Forest Gateau, a notorious relic from dinner-party menus of the 1970s, but actually dating from the 1930s. The Black Forest Gateau cake is more *Cabaret* and Liza Minnelli, all sheer stockings and glossy red lipstick, than sweet trollies in suburban restaurants and Alison Steadman in *Abigail's Party*.

Preheat the oven to 170°C (gas 3). Grease and flour the tins, or grease and base-line them with parchment paper.

In a stand mixer or by hand in a bowl, beat the butter until smooth, pale and fluffy, then mix in the flour, cocoa powder, caster sugar, baking powder and salt until well combined.

In a separate bowl, whisk together the milk, eggs and vanilla extract. Pour half of the egg mixture into the butter mixture, beat together, then add the remaining egg mixture and beat together. Tip half of the mixture into each prepared tin and smooth the tops.

Bake for 20–25 minutes, or until the sponges spring back when lightly pressed with a finger. Turn out, invert and leave to cool on a wire rack.

Skewer the cool cakes all over and pour half the kirsch all over the holes of each cake. The liquid will soak into the sponges.

Whip the cream to soft peaks.

Place the first cake on a plate and spread a third of the whipped cream on to it, leaving a border all around so that it doesn't squirt everywhere when you put the top on.

Add half of the drained black cherries and then top with the second sponge layer, spreading the rest of the cream over the top of the cake. Top with the rest of the black cherries, then the fresh cherries (stack them artfully in a pyramid shape – you want a look of tumbling plenitude.) Dust with the icing sugar and devour.

Rainbow Cake

Serves 10–12

530g plain flour, plus extra for dusting
1 tsp sea salt
230g unsalted butter, softened, plus extra
    for greasing
600g caster sugar
4 large eggs
A few drops of vanilla extract
480ml buttermilk, or natural yoghurt
    mixed with a little crème fraîche
2 tsp white wine vinegar
2 tsp bicarbonate of soda
Food colouring, preferably paste
    or powder, in seven colours
Food flavourings/essences for each colour,
    see intro (optional)

FOR THE ICING
450g cream cheese
500g mascarpone
A few drops of vanilla extract
240g icing sugar
600ml double cream
Edible white 'disco' glitter or
    multicoloured Skittles, for decoration
    (optional)

EQUIPMENT
2 or more 18cm sandwich tins (if you
    only have 20cm tins, your layers will be
    thinner, with 250g cake batter in each)
7 bowls

This is the cake I demonstrated on BBC Radio 4's Woman's Hour in 2011. Not many people had heard of it then, but it's now quite common. It's still a marvellous cake for both children's and adults' tea parties. Watch children's faces (and adults' too!) when you cut into the cake and reveal the rainbow slices.

Traditionally, to follow the colours of a rainbow, it would have seven layers: red, orange, yellow, green, blue, indigo and violet (though in the picture on the right I got carried away and used eight!). You can make more colours by mixing those you have, for example, red and blue make violet, some yellow in the green gives you a different shade of green. Use food colouring paste or powder rather than ordinary liquid food colouring: they make the sponge batter more stable. You can play with the colours like paint pots. Really fun to do with the kids!

You need 18cm sandwich cake tins for this recipe. I only have two so I bake two layers at a time, but if you have more, even better! Each time you bake you will need to grease and flour the tins, or you could line them with parchment paper instead.

You could also add flavouring such as lemon essence for the yellow layer, orange essence for the orange layer, peppermint extract for the green, almond extract for a pale green, and unsweetened cocoa powder for the brown.

Preheat the oven to 170°C (gas 3). Grease and flour your cake tins, or grease and base-line them with parchment paper.

Sift the flour and salt together in a bowl.

Using a stand mixer or wooden spoon by hand in a bowl, beat the butter until whipped. It should be spread fluffily around the sides of your mixing bowl. Add the caster sugar and beat for 5 minutes.

In a separate bowl, whisk the eggs and then add them to the sugar/butter mixture in a slow trickle while whisking. Add 1–2 teaspoons of the flour at the same time. You want to try to prevent curdling that would make a dent in your sponge. Every so often, stop the mixer and scrape down the sides. The mixture should look pale and airy. Add the vanilla extract and stir in.

Take the remaining flour and the buttermilk or yoghurt and add alternately to your mixture, ending with flour. This should be beaten in on low speed or gently by hand.

In another bowl, mix the vinegar and bicarbonate of soda together and add to the main mixture. Mix until fully incorporated. Now you have your sponge batter.

Take seven bowls and divide the mixture evenly between them. Stir a different food colouring and flavouring, if using, into each one.

Transfer the mixtures to your prepared cake tins and bake for 20–25 minutes, until a skewer inserted into the sponges comes out clean. The layers are thinner than in a normal sponge sandwich so use a fish slice to turn out the sponges on to a wire rack. Leave to cool for a couple of minutes, then cover with parchment paper to prevent them drying out. Repeat as necessary until you have 7 baked sponge layers. Leave them to cool completely.

While the sponge layers are cooling, make the icing. In a bowl, beat together the cream cheese and mascarpone. Add the vanilla extract and icing sugar and mix. In a separate bowl, whip the double cream to form soft peaks and then fold it into the cheese mixture until combined.

Assemble the sponge layers in the order of your choice, spreading a layer of the cream cheese icing between each layer. Then, with a palette knife, 'crumb coat' the cake by spreading a thin layer of icing all over the outside. Put the cake in the fridge for an hour or two to chill (but don't chill the remaining icing, otherwise it may firm up too much), then spread the rest of the icing thickly all over the cake, completely covering the top and sides.

Sprinkle some white 'disco' glitter or multicoloured Skittles on top, if you like.

Meringues

Swan Pavlovas

Makes 1 swan pavlova (serves 1-2)

2 egg whites
100g caster sugar
¼ tsp cream of tartar
100ml double cream
25g slivered blanched almonds
6 silvered sugared almonds (optional)

EQUIPMENT
Disposable piping bag

The pavlova was named after the legendary Russian ballerina Anna Pavlova during her tour of Australia and New Zealand in the early 20th century. Both countries fight over whose dish it is. Anna Pavlova's greatest role was as the dying swan. Anna wasn't the best technical dancer, but her slim ankles, delicate long limbs and frail demeanour entranced audiences. Enjoy the pale fragility of this snowy meringue. Make several necks, as they snap easily, and at least two sets of wings. The body should be slightly hollow to accommodate the billowing tutu of cream. I make these in all sizes but it's nice to have mini ones too (see opposite).

Preheat the oven to 110°C (gas ¼). Line 2 baking sheets with parchment paper.

Pour the egg whites into a clean bowl and start to whisk. Whisk until the egg whites become thick, then gradually add the caster sugar, then the cream of tartar. Keep whisking until you have stiff peaks.

Prop the piping bag in a jug and scrape the meringue into it. Snip off the tip of the bag and pipe out the base of the swan, an oval with raised sides, on a prepared baking sheet (I piped mine about 15cm long and 10cm wide, but pipe yours out to the size you want). Bake for 1–1¼ hours or until you can easily remove the meringue from the baking sheet and the bottom remains intact. Leave to cool completely on the baking sheet.

While the base is baking, draw a template of wings and necks on your parchment paper on the second baking sheet. Make extras so you have spares, as they are fragile and break easily. Pipe out two sets of triangular wings (about 10 x 4cm) and several S-shaped necks (about 8 x 2cm), trying to make them equal lengths and sizes. Pipe forward 'S' and backward 'S' shapes so that you can stick them together.

Bake the wings and necks for 30–45 minutes, checking occasionally to make sure they don't brown. Leave to cool completely on the baking sheet.

Whip the cream to stiff peaks and spoon it into the hollow of the meringue base. Carefully position the two wings (one set) and 2 neck/head halves into the cream. Stud the cream with silvered sugared almonds (if using) and the slivered blanched almonds (so that they look like feathers). Serve immediately.

Chocolate

A Word About Cooking with Chocolate

The easiest way to melt chocolate is to use a microwave if you have one. ONLY melt the chocolate in 30-second bursts (on full power). Don't think, oh I'll do it for a minute because it's quicker: the chocolate will seize up and be unusable. Good-quality chocolate is expensive, so you don't want to waste it. If you don't have a microwave, then you can melt chocolate in a bain-marie – a heatproof bowl set over a pan of gently simmering water. But, the bottom of the bowl must not touch the water underneath.

I'm not a chocolate snob: I prefer milk chocolate (Cadbury, probably because I grew up with it) to dark chocolate generally, but in cooking you get better results with dark chocolate. Green and Black's and supermarket own-brand dark chocolates are pretty good. My favourite, however, is an Italian brand, Amedei, which, while being really high in cocoa solids, isn't too bitter (see page 250 for stockists). Look for dark chocolate containing at least 70 per cent cocoa solids.

White chocolate, technically not chocolate at all for it contains no cocoa solids, is the hardest to work with and will seize up easily. Make sure you buy the best quality you can find as it will be more forgiving.

'Couverture' is what professional bakers use. It has a high proportion of cocoa butter, which makes it easier to work with. You can buy it online. See the directory on page 250 for stockists.

Tempering is a technique for making sure the chocolate is shiny rather than dull and has a clean snap when you break it. It's all to do with molecules. One way to temper is to keep back 30 per cent when melting your chocolate, then stir in the 30 per cent at the end. Make sure it doesn't get splashed with water.

Chocolate
Dark chocolate shouldn't be heated over 32°C.
Milk chocolate shouldn't go over 30°C.
White chocolate shouldn't go over 29°C.

Chocolate Teacups

Makes 8

A little grapeseed oil

300g extra bitter dark chocolate, chopped
(this allows for a little extra, as you only
need about 33g for each cup and saucer
– 70% cocoa solids Lindt Excellence is
a good choice)

About 400ml coffee ice cream (or vanilla
or chocolate ice cream, if you prefer)

1 can (250g) ready-whipped cream
(squirty cream), chilled

Unsweetened cocoa powder, to dust

8 tiny Walnut Macaroons (see page 148),
to serve

EQUIPMENT

8 china saucers (coffee cup saucer size)

8 thin acetate strips (see stockists on page 250)

Ultra-clean, dry chocolate brush or a
clean, very small artist's paintbrush
(or a squeaky clean pastry brush)

8 rings cut from ordinary plastic plumbing
pipe (about 4–5cm high and 2–3cm in
diameter) – make sure it's squeaky clean
before you use it

Small piping bag fitted with a 5mm
plain nozzle

My mum's friend Joy is a talented amateur pastry chef. She learnt with the best at the restaurant of Raymond Blanc. These chocolate teacups are such an elegant idea for an afternoon tea. Here is Joy's step-by-step guide to how to make them. They are very fragile so take care at all stages. May I suggest you buy coffee ice cream to fill the little cups?

Before you start, clear the bottom shelf of the fridge. Lightly oil the undersides of the saucers with grapeseed oil and then cover each one tightly and smoothly with a square of cling film, large enough to cover the whole saucer (with enough slack to be able to twist the edges together tightly on the top side of the saucer in order to have a grip on the saucer), thus creating a perfectly smooth cling-filmed underside to each saucer. Set aside.

Melt the chocolate in a bain-marie (see page 69), making sure the bowl doesn't touch the simmering water underneath.

Lay an acetate strip on some kitchen paper and brush it with melted chocolate to 2mm thick using the chocolate or paint brush (or pastry brush), leaving 2cm at one end uncovered. Hold the uncoated edge of the acetate strip with the chocolate facing inwards, bend the strip to form a ring that slightly overlaps and then slide it inside a ring of plastic plumbing pipe. The uncoated side of the acetate strip will be against the inside wall of the plumbing pipe. Check the chocolate coating inside is even, touching it up with the brush if necessary, and then refrigerate. Repeat with the remaining acetate strips and rings of plastic plumbing pipe. Refrigerate until set.

Brush the melted chocolate on to the undersides of the prepared saucers until it is 1mm thick. Run a thumb around the edge to give it a clean edge; you should be able to see the rim of the saucer. Refrigerate immediately.

Put some melted chocolate into the piping bag and pipe 8 handle shapes on to parchment paper. Chill in the fridge.

Once the chocolate has set, transfer all the parts to plastic boxes or trays and leave them in the fridge overnight.

The following day, very carefully remove the plastic plumbing pipe ring only from each cup. Do not remove the acetate strip. Very, very carefully remove the china saucers by opening the twisted knot of cling film and using hand heat only on the underside of each saucer. Gently release the cling-filmed chocolate saucer from the china saucer. Keep the cling film on each chocolate saucer (this is so it doesn't have contact with the air, which gives it a tempered shiny look).

When you're ready to assemble your cups and saucers, have ready the ice cream, the chilled can of whipped (squirty) cream, an empty shelf in the fridge, a little leftover melted chocolate for 'glue' and repairs, cold dessert plates, the cocoa powder and macaroons. You need to work with cold hands.

To assemble each chocolate teacup, remove 1 cup, 1 saucer and 1 handle from the fridge and remove the ice cream from the freezer. Put a blob of melted chocolate on a chilled serving plate. Carefully remove the cling film from the chocolate saucer and stick the saucer on to the plate using the blob of chocolate. Carefully remove the acetate from the chocolate cup and place the cup on the saucer.

Dip the edge of the handle into the melted chocolate and glue it to the side of the cup. Add a small scoop of coffee ice cream to the cup. Pipe whipped cream into the cup over the top of the ice cream. Put the plate in the fridge, and then continue in the same way with the next cup and saucer, until all are assembled.

When you're ready to serve, remove all the saucers from the fridge. Shake a little cocoa powder over the cream, put a few little macaroons to the side of each saucer and serve immediately.

Tip: When assembling the chocolate teacups, you'll need to work quickly but carefully. You may like to try making just one or two cups, saucers and handles to begin with, before you embark on making all 8.

Tip: The chocolate components (i.e. cups, saucers and handles) can be made and kept in the fridge for a week or so. Once assembled, they should be served immediately.

Walnut Macaroons

Makes lots

100g ground walnuts (whizz your own
 from walnut pieces, pre-ground are
 dark, bitter and too fine)
1 rounded tsp ground rice
100g golden caster sugar
1 large egg white

EQUIPMENT
Piping bag fitted with a small (1.5cm)
 plain nozzle

This is Joy's recipe for walnut macaroons to accompany your Chocolate Teacups (see page 146).

Preheat the oven to 150°C (gas 2). Line a baking sheet with parchment paper or a silicone mat.

Mix together the ground walnuts, ground rice and sugar. Stir in the egg white until smooth. Put the mix into the piping bag and pipe tiny 1.5cm blobs on to the prepared baking sheet as you would for petits fours. Leave some room between each one for the blobs to spread.

Bake for 15 minutes or until they start to turn golden, then remove from the oven and leave to cool completely on the baking sheet.

These can be eaten fresh, or can be frozen between layers of greaseproof paper for up to 1 month. They have the advantage of also being delicious eaten from frozen. Larger blobs make good biscuits, which are great partially dipped in melted chocolate, or sandwiched together with whipped cream or coffee-flavoured cream.

Chocolate Balloon Bowls

Enough balloons for your guests (one each)
Approximately 20g chocolate per 'bowl'
A freezer
Your breath to blow up the balloons!

This is a fun idea for making edible bowls, which you can use for ice cream or chocolate truffles. Clear a shelf or two in the freezer prior to making them. (It's a chance to have a good clear-out, too!)

Blow up the quantity of balloons required, not too big (imagine an individual bowl-size). Break a good-quality bar of dark, milk or white chocolate into pieces (allow about 20g chocolate per balloon) and melt it in a bowl in the microwave (on full power) in 30-second bursts (NEVER longer, or it seizes), or in a bain-marie (see page 69), making sure the bowl doesn't touch the simmering water underneath.

Dip each balloon bottom in the melted chocolate, then transfer it to a baking sheet lined with parchment paper or a silicone mat. Freeze for several hours until firm, then pop the balloons. Serve the chocolate bowls immediately, filled with ice cream or truffles.

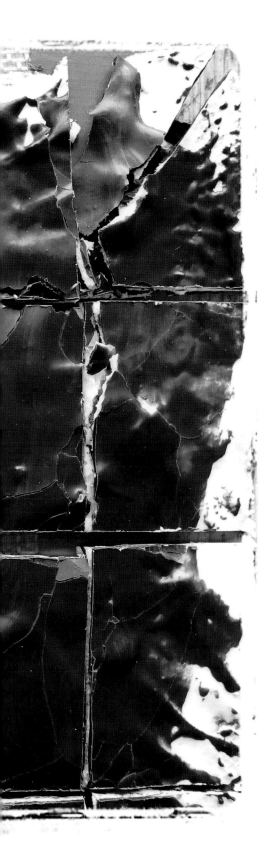

Home–made After Ates

Makes 20–30 squares

1 egg white
300g icing sugar
Juice of ½ lemon
A large bunch of fresh mint leaves, very finely chopped
A few drops of peppermint extract
400g good-quality dark chocolate, broken into pieces
Fresh mint leaves, to decorate

A food that comes in its own little packets is always a joy, particularly After Eights. Is there a kid that hasn't descended in the morning after the parents' dinner party to rifle through the dark satiny envelopes to see if there are any chocolates left?

So, I made my own version of After Eights, during the process of which I had a revelation. The name After Eight doesn't just refer to the hour after which they can be eaten, it's also a wordplay: 'After Ate'. After you've eaten... geddit?

In a bowl, whisk the egg white until it is stiff. Add the icing sugar, lemon juice, chopped mint and peppermint extract and mix to make a fondant. Using a spatula, spread the fondant over parchment paper or a silicone mat to 2mm thickness. Leave to dry.

Melt half of the chocolate in a bowl in the microwave (on full power) in 30-second bursts, or melt it in a bain-marie (see page 69), making sure the bowl doesn't touch the simmering water underneath.

Once the top of the fondant is dry, pour the chocolate over the top, smoothing with a rubber spatula. Leave it to dry for a couple of hours, then carefully flip over the parchment paper or silicone mat and carefully peel it off the fondant. Set aside until touch dry.

Melt the rest of the chocolate as before and then smooth it over the top of the fondant, to cover the fondant completely. Leave to dry, then cut into squares.

You can use old After Eight envelopes or serve as is. Decorate with mint leaves. These will keep for up to 2 weeks in an airtight container.

White-chocolate-dipped Physalis

1 pummet physallis fruit
100g white chocolate
Patterned Chocolate transfer sheet of your
  choice (see stockists page 250)

These small orange sweet and sour fruit, housed in delicate husks like Chinese lanterns, are fantastic for decorating cakes and puddings. You can dip other fruit, such as strawberries, but I love the way that the sour physalis knock back the very sweet white chocolate. Use these as a decoration for any desserts or cakes. I use it to top my Passion Fruit Cloud Cake (see page 124). Simply pull back the husks of the fruit, twist and then dip the fruits into melted white chocolate, then leave them to dry.

Add pattern for extra decoration using a chocolate transfer sheet, available from kitchenware shops and online (see stockists on page 250). Once you've dipped the physalis into the chocolate, leave them to dry on the transfer sheet. It's a simple trick to make your desserts look professional and creative.

Fig and Chocolate Tart

Serves 8–10

175g salted butter, softened,
  plus extra for greasing
75g caster sugar
2 egg yolks
150g chestnut flour
100g type '00' pasta flour,
  plus extra for dusting
20g unsweetened cocoa powder

FOR THE FILLING
200g good-quality dark chocolate,
  finely chopped
200ml double cream
200g light muscovado sugar
4 fresh figs, cut in half
Unsweetened cocoa powder or icing sugar,
  for dusting

EQUIPMENT
36 x 12cm rectangular loose-based tart tin
  (or 20cm square loose-based tart tin)
Baking beans or beads

This rich recipe uses chestnut flour, which is available in Italian food shops, delis and online (see stockists on page 250). It's sweet and soft. Replace with plain flour or Italian type '00' flour if it's too hard to get hold of, but I think it makes a lovely combination with the dark chocolate, seasonal figs and perhaps a small liqueur to imbibe. A perfect autumn dish (see picture overleaf).

Cream together the butter and caster sugar until light and fluffy. Add the egg yolks, mix to combine, then add the two flours and cocoa powder. Mix well, then flatten into a disc, cover with cling film and chill in the fridge for 1 hour.

Preheat the oven to 180°C (gas 4). Grease and flour the tart tin.

Lightly dust your worktop with flour and roll out the pastry to 3–5mm thickness. Curl it over your rolling pin and lay it in the prepared tart tin, if it breaks press it in with your fingers. Trim around the rim of the tart tin and prick the bottom several times with a fork. Cover the tart base with a piece of greaseproof paper and then a layer of baking beans.

Bake for 20 minutes or until the pastry looks cooked. Remove from the oven.

Meanwhile, for the filling, melt the chocolate, cream and muscovado sugar in a bowl in the microwave (on full power) in 30-second bursts, or melt it in a bain-marie (see page 69), making sure that the bowl doesn't touch the simmering water underneath. Mix together until shiny and thick. Pour the mixture into the warm tart shell and then place the fig halves, cut sides up, in the chocolate mixture at regular intervals, pressing them down gently.

Bake for 8 minutes or until the top is lightly set.

Serve warm or cold, dusted with cocoa powder or icing sugar.

Jubilant Jellies

Even at an adults' afternoon tea, with airs and graces and fine manners, there is still a little bit of kid in us that yearns for our childhood favourites of jelly and ice cream. The pleasure of jelly is in the mouthfeel: sweet, cold and wobbly.

To work out how much liquid your mould/bowl holds, fill it with water, then pour the water into a measuring jug. This way you know how much jelly to make. Try to use a flexible jelly mould as it makes it so much easier to get the jelly out. If your mould isn't a standard size, you need approximately 1 gelatine leaf to 100ml of liquid (a little less if you aren't unmoulding), so adjust the recipe as necessary.

There are different types of gelatine, I tend to use platinum gelatine leaves that you can buy in most supermarkets. For commercial use, there is a bronze grade but you won't need that. Platinum gives a clearer, cleaner look to your jelly. One can also use powdered gelatine, and some professional pastry chefs swear by it.

Here is a conversion table for powdered gelatine to leaves (courtesy of chef Madalene Bonvini-Hamel, who writes the blog The British Larder):

• 1 level teaspoon of powdered gelatine = 1½ leaves
• 3 level teaspoons of powdered gelatine = 3 leaves
• 6 level teaspoons of powdered gelatine = 6 leaves

Always cover your gelatine leaves sufficiently with cold water when soaking, or they can stick together and create lumps.

Below is a handy gelatine-to-water ratio table that I nicked from famous jelly mongers Bompas & Parr.

Gelatine-to-Water Ratio

Mould volume	Unmoulding jelly	Not unmoulding jelly
300ml	3 leaves gelatine	2.2 leaves gelatine
400ml	4	2.9
500ml	5	3.6
600ml	6	4.36
700ml	7	5
800ml	8	5.7
900ml	9	6.4
1 litre	10	7.1

Jelly made with gelatine, like chocolate, melts at body temperature, which is why it has such a seductive mouthfeel. It should be kept in the fridge until just before serving, as it will last only a couple of hours maximum out of the fridge before it starts to melt.

For strict vegetarians, you can use agar agar in place of gelatine, but it doesn't taste as nice, being slightly more granular. Gelatine leaves must be softened in cold water then gently heated, whereas agar agar is boiled. The latter is easier to handle and more stable. I don't eat meat but I eat jelly made with gelatine; I like to remain in denial that gelatine is made from animal hooves.

Agar agar is a vegetarian alternative to jelly. Like carrageenan, another gelling agent, it is made from seaweed. The downside is it doesn't have the melt-in-the-mouth quality of jelly. Bompas & Parr told me that the entire jelly 'industry' is on a quest to make a vegetarian version that dissolves at body temperature and has the same mouthfeel as gelatin. 'The person that invents this will become a multi-millionaire', Sam Bompas told me.

Agar agar comes in powder or flakes. The powder often comes in 7g sachets and can be bought in many Chinese shops, health food shops or online. Or, it is available in flake form from Clearspring. Dr Oetker also does 'vege-gel' made from carrageenan, which works in a similar fashion.

Agar agar dissolves in hot water, unlike jelly which dissolves in cold water.

You sprinkle the agar agar powder into hot water and then bring it to the boil, this activates the thickening agent. It can take 10 minutes to dissolve. A 7g sachet will be correct for 600ml of liquid.

Agar agar sets more firmly than gelatine and does not require chilling.

Overleaf is a sophisticated jelly that will make your guests gasp with pleasure.

Alcoholic Clementine Jelly with Gold Leaf

Serves 4–6

5 platinum gelatine leaves (see page 156)
450ml clementine or orange juice
50g caster sugar
50ml Cointreau/triple sec liqueur or any
    orange liqueur
1–2 sheets of gold leaf, broken into pieces
    (or a little pot of gold scraps such as you
    get in the supermarket)
5 clementines, peeled and segmented
    (try to remove as much of the white
    membranes as you can, the segments
    will look prettier in the jelly)

EQUIPMENT
1 jelly mould or bowl
    (at least 500ml volume)
Clean small artist's paintbrush

I first made this for Christmas teatime. It was a lovely light dessert, tangy and refreshing. It also felt sort of non-calorific somehow, almost like a health food after all the heavy stuff of Christmas lunch.

First of all, decide what you are going to present the jelly in: a mould or in a bowl? A mould will be turned out, therefore make sure you put the gold leaf in first. With a bowl, the gold leaf goes in last as you aren't turning it out (see picture page 157).

Soak the gelatine leaves in a bowl of cold water (see tip below). Squeeze out the water, then put them in a bain-marie (see page 69) and cover with the fruit juice. Add the caster sugar and very gently heat until the sugar and gelatine have dissolved. Remove from the heat and stir in the Cointreau or triple sec.

If you are using a mould, scrunch up some foil on a tray and up-end the mould on to it. Pour a thin layer of jelly, about 5mm depth, into the mould or bowl. Using the paintbrush, transfer the gold leaf pieces into the thin jelly layer at the bottom of the mould or bowl (see tip below). Pour in some more jelly to about 3cm depth, followed by some of the clementine segments, and then put it in the fridge to set, about 30 minutes. Once set, add half of the remaining jelly and more clementine segments. Return to the fridge to set again. Repeat as necessary, until you have used up all the jelly and most of the clementine segments (you need to keep a few clementine segments for decoration), ending with some clementine segments floating in the jelly. Return to the fridge to set completely.

After 4–6 hours you can unmould the jelly, if using a mould (or simply serve it from the bowl). Wet your presentation plate beforehand so that you can position the jelly, then unmould the jelly on to it. Decorate with the remaining clementine segments and serve.

Salted Caramel Lollies with Home-made Sherbet Dib-dabs

Makes 20

This recipe is both fun and easy. Making the lollies from salted caramel transforms them into an adult delight.

100ml light corn syrup
  (see stockists on page 250)
2 tbsp water
1½ tsp white wine vinegar
150g caster sugar
10g fleur de sel or good-quality sea salt
200g unsalted butter, cubed
1 tsp vanilla extract

FOR THE SHERBERT
100g icing sugar
2 tsp citric acid
2 tsp bicarbonate of soda

EQUIPMENT
Sugar thermometer
Lollipop sticks

Line a baking sheet with parchment paper or a silicone mat.

Put the corn syrup, water, vinegar, sugar and salt into a pan over a medium heat and heat, shifting the pan until the sugar melts, then add the butter. Heat the mixture to 150°C, brushing the inside of the pan with water to prevent crystallisation. Once you have the desired temperature, take the pan off the heat and add the vanilla extract. Leave for a couple of minutes to cool so that the mixture thickens.

Carefully (I got a big blister when I did this, so use a long-handled metal spoon) spoon circles of the hot caramel on to the prepared baking sheet, making each one about 3.5cm in diameter. Press the end of a lolly stick (about 2cm) into each circle of caramel and rotate the stick slightly so that the stick is covered with cara-mel. Leave to set.

Mix together the sherbet ingredients. That's it. Add more icing sugar if you want more sweetness and dip away.

4. Themed Teas

I must 'fess up, I'm a supporter of an activity generally known as styling. How else to describe it? Accessorising? Fluffing? Zhooshing? Decorating? Primping? Basically, arranging and dressing things up. No verb properly covers this intrinsically feminine urge, which in pregnancy is referred to as 'nesting', and classically occurs during the fifth month. It's hormonally driven. There are worse addicts than me: I've gone on holiday with friends who restyle their hotel rooms! Even at backpackers' hostels! Even their tents when camping! They start throwing scarves over lamps or covering their sleeping bags with sarongs.

Doing a themed afternoon tea party is a major opportunity to style it up. I have four suggested themes here, but feel free to come up with your own ideas, these are just to start you off.

Midwinter Night's Dream Afternoon Tea

his is a very floral and woodlandy tea, with maybe a little bit of foraged stuff thrown in for good measure. Other suggestions, depending on the season, might be mushroom pies, nettle pesto sarnies, small 'nests' of dyed quail's eggs, or rosehip syrup cocktails.

STYLING TIPS:

Use beautiful dried autumn leaves, flowers, wild berries.

Bird's nests, acorns and moss to decorate the table.

Think hobbits, old-fashioned English cakes, comfort food.

Use flowery linen napkins, tied with twine, threaded with herbs.

Wooden and bone tableware look good, as do English vintage ceramics in the style of Clarice Cliff.

Pots of honey, roasted chestnuts, pine-scented candles.

Menu

Savoury

Seed- or Herb-encrusted Sandwiches	*see page 32*
Rose Butter	*see page 44*

Sweet

Hobbit Seed Cake	*see opposite*
Swedish Saffron Buns or Cat's Eyes	*see page 166*
Woodland Apple Pie	*see page 168*

Centrepiece

Magic Meringue Mushrooms	*see page 170*
The Gingerbread Cottage	*see page 172*

Drinks

Mulled Wine	*see page 177*
Flower Teas	*see page 228*

Hobbit Seed Cake

Serves 8–10

250g self-raising flour
A pinch of sea salt
150g unsalted butter, softened,
    plus extra for greasing
150g caster sugar
3 large eggs
1 tsp vanilla extract
2 tbsp milk
2 tbsp caraway seeds,
    plus extra for sprinkling
3 tbsp poppy seeds (optional)
2–3 tbsp soft light brown sugar,
    for sprinkling

EQUIPMENT
Deep 23cm round loose-based cake tin

Seed cake is both old fashioned and literary. It's been mentioned in Dickens (*David Copperfield*), *Jane Eyre* by Charlotte Brontë, Arthur Ransom's *Swallows and Amazons* and JRR Tolkein's *The Hobbit*. Seed cake was an essential element in the 'second breakfast'. I created a hobbit-themed meal in a yurt in Highgate, north London, complete with wood burner and guests dressed as elves and dwarves.

Here is my recipe for it. Nigel Slater says not to add too many caraway seeds and I agree with him. You want a hint, not to be overwhelmed. You could also add poppy seeds if you want it extra seedy (see picture overleaf).

Preheat the oven to 180°C (gas 4). Grease and line the cake tin with parchment paper.

In a bowl, sift together the flour and salt. In a separate bowl, cream together the butter and caster sugar until pale in colour. Beat in the eggs, one at a time, followed by the vanilla extract, ensuring it is thoroughly incorporated. Then gradually add the flour, a bit at a time, followed by the milk. Gently stir in the caraway seeds, and poppy seeds, if using.

Spoon the mixture into the prepared cake tin and level the top. Bake for 50 minutes or until a skewer inserted into the centre of the cake comes out clean.

Once ready, remove from the oven and sprinkle immediately with caraway seeds and brown sugar. Leave to cool in the tin for 10 minutes, then remove the cake from the tin and place on a wire rack to cool completely.

Serve in slices, and feel free to spread thickly with butter.

PEEK
BISCUIT

Swedish Saffron Buns or Cat's Eyes

Makes 30–40

A pinch of saffron strands
140g caster sugar, plus 1 tsp
450ml milk
1kg plain flour, plus extra for dusting
½ tsp sea salt
21g (3 x 7g sachets) fast-action dried yeast
225g quark/soured cream/crème fraîche,
   at room temperature
140g unsalted butter, softened
Raisins, for finishing
   (you'll need about 60–80)
Egg wash, for glazing

Scandinavian baking recipes often use exotic spices such as cinnamon, cardamom or saffron, brought back by Viking exploration. This is a typical mid-winter recipe, leading up to the 21st of December, the shortest day, when warmth and light are most desired. These yellow S-shaped buns are cheering. In the UK, we have a Cornish equivalent known as Revel Buns.

Crush the saffron strands with 1 teaspoon of the sugar using a pestle and mortar. Warm the milk in a pan and add the saffron to it. Stir it, turn off the heat and set aside until lukewarm.

Put the flour, the remaining 140g sugar, the salt and yeast into a bowl. In a separate large bowl, mix together the lukewarm milk and the quark or soured cream/crème fraîche. Gradually add the flour mixture to the milk mixture and stir until a dough forms. Knead the dough on a lightly floured work surface until it's elastic. If you're using a stand mixer, add the butter until it's all incorporated. Otherwise, knead in the butter until incorporated.

Put the dough into a large bowl, cover and leave to rise in a warm place for about 40 minutes or until doubled in size. To improve lightness, after 20 minutes, fold the risen dough into thirds to make a narrow rectangle, then turn it 90 degrees and fold it in thirds again. Leave it to rise for the remaining 20 minutes.

Line a couple of baking sheets with parchment paper or silicone mats.

Turn the dough out on to a lightly floured work surface and cut it into 30–40 equal pieces. Roll out the pieces with your hands into snakes, each about 20cm long, then flatten them slightly with a rolling pin. Roll each strip inwards from either end to make S shapes, and prod a raisin into the middle of each coiled end (so two per 'S'). Lay them on the prepared baking sheets, cover and leave to rise in a warm place for a further 30 minutes.

Preheat the oven to 240°C (gas 9).

Brush the risen rolls with egg wash and bake for 8–12 minutes, until golden. Transfer to a wire rack to cool, then serve.

Woodland Apple Pie

Serves 6–8

400g plain flour, plus extra for dusting
1 tsp sea salt
200g cold unsalted butter, grated,
    plus extra for greasing
Cold water, for mixing
1kg mixed cooking and eating apples
    (whatever you have to hand), peeled, cored
    and quartered (from 1.5kg unpeeled)
3 tbsp demerara, light muscovado
    or soft light brown sugar, plus extra for
    sprinkling
1½ tsp ground ginger
2–3 tbsp Calvados apple brandy (optional)
1 egg yolk mixed with a couple of drops of
    milk, for glazing

EQUIPMENT
23cm round deep pie dish
Leaf and flower cutters

OPTIONAL ACCOMPANIMENT
300ml crème fraîche
25ml Calvados
2–3 tbsp icing sugar

*For the optional accompaniment,
simply combine all the ingredients to
make the sweetened Calvados-infused
crème fraîche.*

To create a woodland look, I used leaf and flower cutters to make the pattern on top of this apple pie. Then I rolled small pieces of pastry to make the 'stems'. I've added Calvados here as it is an apple brandy, but it is optional. Using a mix of cooking and eating apples gives acidity, sweetness and a good texture.

Preheat the oven to 180°C (gas 4). Grease the pie dish.

Sift the flour and salt into a large mixing bowl or just run a fork through to break up the flour and add air. Add the grated butter and use your fingertips to gently work the butter into the flour and salt until the mixture resembles breadcrumbs. Add a few drops of water and gently mix with your hands until the dough comes together. (Alternatively, use a food processor to make the dough.)

Split the dough into 2 flattened discs, wrap them in cling film and leave to rest in the fridge for about 30 minutes.

Meanwhile, put the apple quarters, brown sugar, ginger and the Calvados, if using, into a medium pan over a medium heat. Simmer, uncovered, for 5 minutes or until the apples are tender. Don't over-cook them as you don't want the apples to be mushy. Remove from the heat and leave to cool completely.

Dust a work surface and rolling pin with flour. Roll out each pastry disc into a round about 5mm thickness. Roll one round over the rolling pin and unroll it over the pie dish, then press the pastry into the bottom and up the sides. Spoon in the apples, packing them in tightly.

Brush the rim of the pastry shell with the egg wash and then unroll the second round of pastry over the top. Trim any excess pastry, then crimp the edges of the pie using a fork.

Now is the time to decorate. Collect all the pastry scraps and roll them out thinly, then cut out shapes using cutters or freehand. Decorate the top of your pie, securing the pastry shapes on top using egg wash, then brush all over with egg wash and make a couple of incisions in the centre, to allow steam to escape. Use a little butter to grease the rim of the pie and sprinkle with brown sugar.

Bake on the bottom shelf of the oven for 40–45 minutes, until golden and firm to the touch.

Serve the pie hot, warm or cold, either with the flavoured crème fraîche or ice cream.

Magic Meringue Mushrooms

Makes 20

2 egg whites
¼ tsp cream of tartar
A pinch of sea salt
120g caster sugar
Dark red (claret) food colouring paste
 (if you want to make magic toadstools)
 (optional)
A stick of hard liquorice candy
 (see stockists on page 250)
100g good-quality dark chocolate,
 broken into pieces
Unsweetened cocoa powder, for dusting
 (optional)

EQUIPMENT
Several disposable piping bags
Pastry brush

Just like Scandinavians, I love liquorice, especially the salty kind. I played around with liquorice meringue recipes, melting liquorice and using essence of liquorice, but all I got was ugly brown meringues. Eventually I figured out the best method is to get some hard liquorice candy and grate it on to the meringue tops. The combination of chocolate and liquorice with the feather-light meringues works very well. Get some disposable piping bags as you are going to be doing a great deal of piping. I've doubled the recipe, so if you mess up a bunch then you have plenty more.

Preheat the oven to 110°C (gas ¼). Lay out as many baking sheets as you possess and line them with parchment paper or silicone mats.

Whisk your egg whites (I hope you have an electric whisk, as this will save on elbow grease!) until they form soft peaks. Add the cream of tartar and salt. Then add the sugar, slowly, while continuing to whisk on high speed. Eventually it should look glossy and stiff.

Using a tall jug or glass to hold your piping bag (folded back so you can get the mixture into the pointy bit), scoop about half of the mixture into the bag. Cut the tip off the end of the bag, but not too big – remember the hole will get bigger as you pipe. If you want to make toadstools, put a quarter of the remaining meringue mixture into another bowl and mix it with some dark red food colouring, if using. Save the rest of the meringue mixture for sticking the stems and caps of the toadstool meringues together (and for adding little white spots to the toadstool caps), if making these. Keep this in an airtight container or another piping bag.

First, pipe your mushroom stems. Holding the piping bag directly over a prepared baking sheet and making sure it's close to the sheet, pipe a sort of cone shape (about 1.5cm across and 2–3cm high). You need about 20. With a wet finger, slightly flatten the top of each one – you need it flat so that it fits on to the cap of the mushroom. Some of the stems will fall over, so pipe extra. You want them straight and upright.

Now, pipe the caps: this is easier. Pipe circular mounds about 5cm across and 2cm high. Again, you need about 20. And again, smooth the top of each one with a wet finger. Finely grate the liquorice candy on top of the caps. Or, for toadstools, using another piping bag, pipe the same size and number of caps (about 20) using the red meringue.

Bake the caps and stems for 45 minutes, making sure they don't go brown.

If you're making toadstools, make a teensy hole at the end of another piping bag, spoon in some of the leftover white meringue and pipe little white spots on top of the red caps, then bake them for a further 15 minutes.

Remove from the oven and leave to cool completely on the baking sheets.

Once they've cooled, you will notice that the bottoms of many of the caps are 'dipped', just like real mushrooms.

Melt your chocolate either in a bain-marie (see page 69), making sure the bowl doesn't touch the simmering water underneath, or in a bowl in the microwave (on full power) in 30-second bursts (in the microwave is the easiest way). Using a pastry brush, paint the dipped underside of your white mushroom caps with melted chocolate, then stick the stems on to the undersides of the caps and leave to dry. Handle with care or they'll break.

For toadstools, use the leftover meringue mixture to stick the stems to the red caps, cap sides down, then place them back on a baking sheet and bake in the oven for 5 minutes until dry. Leave to cool.

If you don't like or cannot get hold of liquorice, dust all the mushrooms (but not the toadstools) with the cocoa powder to give that speckled mushroomy look on top.

If you have any leftover meringue mixture, simply pipe, bake, assemble and decorate some more mushrooms or toadstools in the same way as before.

The Gingerbread Cottage

Makes 1 gingerbread cottage

250g unsalted butter, softened
200g dark muscovado sugar
10 tbsp golden syrup
600g plain flour
2 tsp bicarbonate of soda
4 tsp ground ginger
1 tsp ground allspice
1 tsp ground cinnamon
Boiled sweets in different colours
    (to create the windows)
200g caster sugar and 180ml water,
    for the caramel (see overleaf)
Vegetable oil, for greasing

FOR THE ROYAL ICING
1 egg white
250g icing sugar
A few drops of lemon juice

FOR DECORATION
Red liquorice laces, for the Christmas tree
    'candles' (optional)
2–3 Cadbury Curly Wurly chocolate bars,
    for the fence
Chocolate finger biscuits, for the vegetable
    patch
Oreo cookies, crushed, for the earth
Flower- and vegetable-shaped sweets,
    for the flowers and vegetables
Fizzy laces or mini Daim Bars, for the pathway
1–2 Cadbury Flake bars, or cinnamon
    cassia sticks, for the logs
Icing sugar, to dust

EQUIPMENT
Small heart-shaped cutter (for the windows)
Christmas-tree cutter
Piping bag fitted with a small plain nozzle
Cake board
Heatproof pastry brush
Lots of patience

A gingerbread cottage makes a spectacular centrepiece for a woodland tea. Here are my step-by-step instructions, but you don't have to follow everything I've suggested – think up your own ideas and simply use this as your starting point.

There are several templates available to download from the internet, from simple A-frame houses/cottages to complex colonial-style mansions. It's probably best to start simple. It's essential that the gingerbread pieces bake as flat as possible: this is not just baking, but architecture. Bendy pieces won't fit together.

A gingerbread cottage will last for weeks if kept in a cool, dry place, but do allow your guests to eat it. Once I gave each table a small sparkly hammer to do a demolition job at the end of the meal. I've rarely seen such joy on the faces of adults.

This recipe gives you quite a light gingerbread bake. I've tested several recipes and I found this to be the best. You'll need to start this recipe a couple of days before you plan to serve it.

First, you need to make a very simple gingerbread dough by mixing together the butter, muscovado sugar, golden syrup, flour, bicarbonate of soda and ground spices to make a dough. If it is too dry, add a drop or two of cold water to bring it all together. Separate it into 6 pieces (4 for the walls and 2 for the roof) and flatten each piece into a patty shape. Cover with cling film and refrigerate overnight.

The following day, download a template from the internet, or draw one on paper (opposite is a simple template that you could use as a guide), and cut it out.

Preheat the oven to 180°C (gas 4). Line 2 baking sheets with parchment paper.

Roll out the gingerbread dough on a lightly oiled work surface to 5mm thickness and cut out all the pieces using your template. A little pro-trick is to buy rolling pin 'guides' (see page 66) to help your rolling out stay even.

Lay the gingerbread pieces flat on one of the prepared baking sheets. Place boiled sweets into each window frame. For mine, I used one red and one yellow sweet and cut out one of the windows in a heart shape for a classic Hansel and Gretel look.

Bake for 10–15 minutes, until the gingerbread is golden brown and the sweets have melted to fill the windows. Remove from the oven and leave all the pieces to cool completely on the baking sheet.

Meanwhile, collect the scraps of dough, and roll them out to 5mm thickness. Cut out a door, some Christmas tree shapes and a few spare pieces of gingerbread cottage shapes in case of breakages, and transfer them to the second prepared baking sheet. Bake, as before, for 10–15 minutes, then leave to cool completely on the baking sheet.

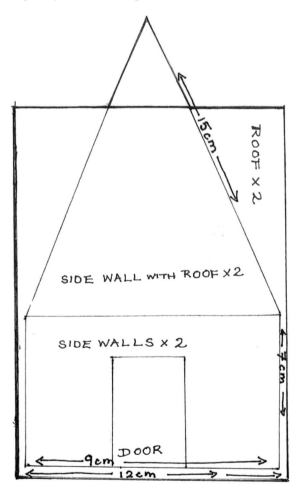

Decorating Your Gingerbread Pieces

Make a royal icing following the instructions on page 71. Double the recipe if you are going to use a lot of icing. Put it straight away into several small airtight containers, as it goes hard with exposure to air.

Prop a disposable (or other) piping bag inside a jug and spoon some of the icing into it. Push it right down to the tip of the bag and roll up the top. If not using a small plain nozzle, use scissors to snip off a tiny bit of the end of the bag (the hole will get bigger as you pipe).

Pipe your icing on to the gingerbread roof, windows and door, using the guidelines below. It takes a little practice to get the pressure and the size of the tip right, but it's great fun. Practice first on a spare bit of gingerbread to make sure the size of the piping hole is just right and increase it if needs be.

To make a pattern that resembles roof tiles (see overleaf), use a 'lasso' motion. Start with a small blob of icing and use it to hook the icing on, then pipe the icing in a U-shaped loop and pin it down with another small blob of icing. Repeat the pattern, joining each 'U' so that it continues in a line across the roof. Continue making lines underneath each other until the whole roof is covered in 'tiles'.

Make sure you pipe the roof 'tiles' the right way round. On an A-frame house/cottage the large roof pieces have the shorter sides at the top and bottom.

To decorate the Christmas trees, pipe around the edge of each biscuit, then pipe wavy lines at a diagonal slant across each tree. I then added tiny pieces of red liquorice lace to my Christmas trees to make 'candles' for the end of the branches (see picture page 176).

Leave it all to dry for 24 hours so that the icing hardens properly, then assemble as given overleaf.

How to Construct Your Gingerbread Cottage

There are two main techniques used to stick ginger-bread pieces together, one using royal icing, the other using caramel. I use the caramel method because it is faster, but it's not as effective when the weather is hot as the caramel tends to melt.

To make the caramel, put the 200g caster sugar and the 180ml water into a medium pan and bring to the boil over a medium heat (give the pan a shake every so often rather than stirring). Reduce the heat to low and simmer until thickened and light brown, about 10 minutes. Remove from the heat and use im-mediately. If it starts to harden during the process of building, gently warm it up again in the pan.

Protect the surface of your table with parchment paper or a silicone mat and place the cake board on top so that you don't have to move your gingerbread cottage once it is stuck together. Move any kids/pets back as caramel is dangerously hot.

Use a jug or cup to prop up the gingerbread pieces and position your four gingerbread walls – the two tall walls opposite each other and the two small walls at either end.

Dip the bottom edge of one of the tall walls into the hot caramel so that it is covered in a thin layer and stick it in place on your cake board. Take one of the small walls and dip the bottom edge and one of its side edges into the hot caramel, then stick it to the cake board and the edge of the secured tall wall. Make sure the edges have contact all the way down. Repeat with the other small wall so you have three walls in place. You can now take the jug away and it should stand on its own.

Don't dip the fourth wall into the caramel. Dip a pastry brush into the hot caramel instead and paint the two edges that will connect the fourth wall to the gingerbread cottage, then attach it to the sides that are already standing so that all four walls are attached. Brush extra caramel on to any corners to secure, as needed. You can do this on the inside of the cottage, to hide any messiness.

Using the pastry brush or a teaspoon, paint or drizzle a layer of hot caramel along the top edges of one side of the cottage. Position one roof piece on to the frame of the cottage. Hold in place until secure, then repeat with the second roof piece. Brush more hot caramel on to the join at the top of the roof to make sure it's really secure. At a later stage, you can pipe some royal icing on to the edges of the cottage to cover up the caramel bonding if you want.

Creating a Woodland Scene

To complete your woodland scene, pipe some icing on to the doorframe and stick the door on to it, so it looks propped open.

Construct a fence around the edge of the board us-ing Curly Wurly bars (they bend slightly), fixing either end to the board with a blob of icing.

Make a vegetable patch with 4 chocolate fingers as 'borders', affixing these with royal icing. Fill the inside with 'earth' made from crushed Oreos. You can make flowers and vegetables out of sweets or use suit-able ready-shaped ones.

Attach your gingerbread Christmas trees to the board using royal icing and then use fizzy laces, one lace either side of the front door, or piece together mini Daim bars, to make a pathway. Make a pile of logs next to the front door with halved Flake bars or cinnamon sticks.

Finally, use a tea strainer to sprinkle the cottage and garden with icing sugar. This covers up a multi-tude of sins and gives a romantic look to your finished gingerbread cottage (see picture overleaf).

Mulled Wine

Serves 8-10

2 bottles (75cl each) red wine
2 oranges, sliced
250g kumquats, halved
2 cinnamon sticks
3 whole cloves
1 star anise
250g sugar (any kind)

I sold this at The Underground Christmas Market at my house in London. (Yes you name it, I've done it from my house: supper clubs, tea parties, brunches, markets, conferences, a home bakery, I'm a cottage industry.) Some guests said it was the best they'd ever had.

I give my recipe below, but I must admit I had a batch on the go on the black enamel surround of the Aga for several weeks. Every time I walked past, I would sling in the remnants of a bottle of booze, a few whole cloves, a handful of sugar or another stick of cinnamon. Last weekend I added the leftovers of my caramelised kumquats. Once you've served out the wine you can add more to the pan, just check the balance of sugar to wine and keep going! It's a flexible alcoholic stew!

Put all the ingredients into a large pan and heat through until warm and gently simmering (but don't let it boil), stirring occasionally. Ladle or pour into glasses and serve.

Marie Antoinette Afternoon Tea

I want candy. Didn't you love the film about Marie Antoinette directed by Sophia Coppola? It was a pastel-hued dream of sugar-high ladies and their dyed poodles, gorgeous silk shoes, fripperies, brightly coloured cakes and sweets. Guests could wear towering powdered wigs and pearls, paint on heart-shaped beauty spots and fan themselves while exchanging witticisms across the table. Let them eat brioche!

STYLING TIPS:

- Pastel colours, pale blue and gold, silks, fans, pearls, ribbons.
- Pretty boxes, silver cutlery, chandeliers, crystal glass tableware, silver candle sticks.
- Swags of fabric, lace and roses, tapestry.
- Guests should be encouraged to wear beauty spots, powder their hair with talc.
- Wear wigs, satin shoes, gloves, cameos.

Menu

Savoury

Bread with Chocolate – *Le Gouter*	*see opposite*
Cheesy Gougères	*see page 180*

Sweet

Raspberry and White Chocolate Madeleines	*see page 181*
French Fancies	*see page 184*

Centrepiece

Blancmange for Nostalgic Adults and Poorly Children	*see page 187*
Pastel Croquembouche	*see page 188*
Champagne Rose Jellies	*see page 190*

Drinks

Decorated Sugar Cubes	*see page 234*
Hot Chocolate	*see page 236*
Teapot Bucks Fizz	*see page 240*

Le Gouter

Serves 2

1 fresh, crusty baguette
Butter, for spreading
100g dark chocolate

French people might not get fat, but they love *le gouter*: a long crusty fresh–as–air baguette, split down the side seam with a finger, spread with unsalted butter and squares of dark chocolate. In French parks you'll see smartly dressed pre–school children at tea time, eating these chocolate baguettes.

Cheesy Gougères

Makes 25

125ml milk
75g unsalted butter, plus extra for greasing
A pinch of sea salt
50g plain flour
2 eggs
50g hard cheese (such as Cheddar,
    Emmental, Tomme, Cheshire, etc),
    grated, or blue cheese, crumbled
1 beaten egg mixed with 1 tbsp milk,
    for glazing
20g finely grated fresh Parmesan cheese
Freshly ground black pepper, to taste

EQUIPMENT
Piping bag fitted with a large plain nozzle
    (or a plastic ziplock bag with the corner
    trimmed)

Tip: To avoid deflated puffs, quickly
prod a skewer into the side of each puff
about 5 minutes before they finish baking,
to release steam.

These are best served straight out of the oven. Prepare the batter, pipe them out, then pop them in the oven about 15 minutes before serving.

Preheat the oven to 200°C (gas 6). Grease and line a baking sheet with parchment paper or a silicone mat.

In a small pan, heat the milk, butter, salt and some black pepper together over a low heat until the butter is melted. Quickly dump all the flour into the pan and use a wooden spoon to stir rapidly, incorporating all the flour into the mixture. When you have a smooth dough that comes clean off the sides of the pan, take it off the heat and put it into the bowl of a stand mixer or into another bowl.

Add the eggs, one at a time, mixing until incorporated, then add the hard or blue cheese to the dough, mixing or stirring all the time until it is shiny and smooth. Spoon the mixture into the piping bag.

Pipe little mounds, about 4cm wide and 2–3cm high, on to your prepared baking sheet, leaving 3cm space between each one. Wet your finger with water and smooth down the little tip of each one.

Lightly brush the beaten egg glaze on to the mounds and then dust them with Parmesan.

Bake for 20 minutes or until golden brown and risen.

Serve immediately.

Raspberry and White Chocolate Madeleines

Makes 20–24 small madeleines

2 eggs
75g caster sugar
2 tsp soft dark brown sugar
A pinch of sea salt
90g plain flour, plus extra for dusting
1 tsp baking powder
A few drops of vanilla extract (optional)
90g unsalted butter, melted and cooled,
  plus extra for greasing
1 tbsp clear honey
50g white chocolate, cut into small pieces
50g raspberries, quartered
Icing sugar, for dusting

EQUIPMENT
2 x 12-hole mini madeleine tins
Piping bag fitted with a medium plain nozzle

Exquisite little sponge bites, these are a match made in heaven when served with a nice cup of tea.

Combine the eggs, caster and brown sugars and salt in a bowl. Work lightly with a spatula until light in colour. In a separate bowl, sift together the flour and baking powder and fold gently into the egg mixture with the vanilla extract, if using. Do not overwork the mixture.

Add the cooled melted butter and honey and mix, then cover the bowl with cling film and leave at room temperature for 30 minutes.

Preheat the oven to 200°C (gas 6). Grease and flour the insides of 20–24 of the moulds in the madeleine tins, making sure you get into all the little crannies.

Spoon the madeleine mixture into the piping bag, then pipe the mixture into the prepared tins. Poke a small piece of white chocolate and a raspberry quarter into each one.

Bake for about 5 minutes or until the centres are risen. Do not overcook or they will be too dry. Leave the madeleines to cool in the tins for a couple of minutes, then turn them out on to a wire rack and dust with a little icing sugar. Serve these quickly to enjoy them at their best.

French Fancies

Makes about 25

250g unsalted butter, softened, plus extra
  for greasing
250g caster sugar
Finely grated zest of 1 lemon for lemon
  fancies, or the seeds scraped from
  1 vanilla pod or 1 tsp vanilla extract
  for vanilla fancies
4 large eggs, beaten
250g plain flour
2½ tsp baking powder
A pinch of sea salt
170g apricot jam (preferably smooth,
  no lumps)
Icing sugar, for dusting
1 packet (454g) white marzipan
1 packet (500g) white or pouring fondant
  (see stockists on page 250)
1 tbsp liquid glucose
Food colouring pastes of your choice
Decorations of your choice (sugar flowers,
  edible silver spray or whatever you
  fancy), or Royal Icing (see page 71) for
  piping decorations

FOR THE SYRUP
150g caster sugar
150ml water
75ml fresh lemon juice for lemon fancies,
  or 1 tsp vanilla extract for vanilla fancies

EQUIPMENT
1 perfectly straight-sided deep 20cm
  square cake tin (it needs to be at least
  6cm deep) (see stockists on page 250)
Metal ruler
Palette knife
Bain-marie (see page 69)
32mm cupcake cases – foil ones work well
  (see stockists on page 250)

My friend Michelle Eshkeri, of the Lavender Bakery (see page 251), who used to work at Konditor & Cook, showed me how to make these. Do not on any account buy the powdered icing sugar known as fondant icing sugar (it doesn't work and will not cover the cake sufficiently). Use a packet of white or pouring fondant icing instead (but do not confuse this with ready-to-roll fondant icing). I've given options here for vanilla or lemon fancies.

The cake is easier to work with if made a day ahead or if refrigerated until cold after brushing with the syrup. Fresh sponge is very crumbly.

Preheat the oven to 180°C (gas 4). Grease the cake tin and line it with parchment paper.

Cream the butter, caster sugar and your chosen flavouring together for 10 minutes using a stand mixer or in a bowl by hand using a wooden spoon. Gradually mix in the beaten eggs, scraping down between additions, then add the sifted flour, baking powder and salt, folding in until combined. Transfer the mixture to the prepared cake tin and smooth the top.

Bake for 20–25 minutes or until springy to the touch. Once baked, remove from the oven and leave the cake to cool in the tin for 10 minutes, then turn it out on to a wire rack and leave to cool completely.

While the cake is baking, make the syrup:

First, make the **plain sugar syrup:** combine the sugar and water in a small heavy-based pan over a low heat, stirring occasionally until the sugar has dissolved, then bring the syrup to the boil and boil for 5 minutes or until it thickens slightly. Remove from the heat and leave to cool.

To make the **lemon syrup:** combine 75ml of the cooled plain sugar syrup with the lemon juice.

To make the **vanilla syrup:** stir the vanilla extract into 150ml of the cooled plain sugar syrup.

Reserve any leftover sugar syrup.

Once the cake is cool, use a sharp serrated knife to trim the top and create a level, straight surface that will become the bottom of the fancies – this way they will all be the same height when finished.

Place the cake on top of the upturned cake tin with the good side facing upwards. Make small holes all over the top of the sponge with a skewer and brush the flavoured syrup over the top of the sponge. Cover with cling film and refrigerate overnight.

Protect your work surface with parchment paper and place a wire rack on top.

Warm the apricot jam with a few tablespoons of the leftover sugar syrup in a pan over a medium-low heat until the jam is liquid. Remove from the heat and press through a heatproof sieve with a spoon. Set aside and keep warm.

Dust your work surface with icing sugar, then knead the marzipan until it is malleable. Use a rolling pin to roll out the marzipan to a square slightly bigger than the cake tin and about 3mm thick. Carefully place the baking tin, with the sponge on top, on to the marzipan and cut roughly around the tin with a sharp knife. Remove the baking tin and put it on a flat surface. Using a pastry brush, brush a thin layer of warm jam all over the sponge cake so that the marzipan will stick to the cake. Drape the marzipan over the rolling pin and place it over the top of the sponge. Using a knife and a metal ruler, square off the marzipan-covered cake on two connecting sides, going just far enough into the cake to create a straight edge and taking off as little as possible, shaving off maybe 3–4mm maximum. You want a nice sharp edge to the cake so you can cut very precise squares. (The other two sides of the cake will be trimmed off as you cut out the squares.)

Using the trimmed sides to measure from, with your ruler, mark where the sponge is going to be cut – make marks (in the marzipan) about 3.5cm apart at the top and bottom of the cake at both ends, and use two sets of marks to line the ruler up against when cutting. You will cut 4–6 lines (to make 5–7 rows) in each direction from the trimmed sides, so that when they are cut, you end up with 25 squares or more depending on the size of your tin (and the final two untrimmed sides of the cake will be discarded).

Cut the sponge cake into the marked squares using a small sharp knife. Using a palette knife, thinly spread some warm jam all over the top of the marzipan squares. Don't separate the squares at this stage (this gets done when you dip them later, and they stay more neatly propped against each other).

Gently heat the fondant and liquid glucose with a few tablespoons of the leftover sugar syrup in a bain-marie (see page 69), making sure the bowl doesn't touch the simmering water underneath – the mixture should be smooth, shiny and of a consistency that is just runny but thickly coats the back of a spoon. Remove from the heat. NEVER let it boil, or it will lose its shine. If it gets too hot, allow it to cool a little before dipping. If it's too thick, add another tablespoon of sugar syrup.

If you are using several different colours for the fondant, do one colour at a time. Place some of the fondant into a small bowl, enough so that it is deep enough to dip half a fancy into. Mix in your chosen food colour. If it starts to get too thick, reheat the fondant in the bain-marie, or in a bowl in the microwave (on full power) in 10-second bursts.

Dip the top half (with the marzipan layer on top) of a sponge square into the fondant and use a fork to help scoop it back out. Don't leave it in for too long or the marzipan layer will fall off. Turn it over quickly (so the dipped part is uppermost) and place it on the wire rack, letting the fondant run down the sides of your very straight cubes. Dip a further 4 sponge squares in the same way. Then place each French Fancy into a cupcake case (the fondant should be sticky/tacky at this stage), pressing the sides of the case to the fondant until set. (I always thought they used special square cases, but they use round cases and press them into the shape of the square.) Decorate these 5 dipped squares with sugar flowers, silver spray or whatever you fancy (see picture pages 182–183).

Repeat with the rest of your fancies, working in batches of 5, dipping them in the fondant, placing them into cupcake cases and decorating them, as before, until all are done. (If you are decorating your fancies with royal icing, dip them in fondant in batches of 5, place in the cupcake cases as before, then pipe on your decorations and leave them to dry before serving or storing.)

Tip: If you like, once you have dipped each batch of 5 fancies, placed them into their cupcake cases and decorated them, you can pack them into a larger deep square cake tin (about 25cm square) in a row. Then repeat with the rest of the fancies, working in batches of 5 and packing them into the tin in rows as you work, until all 25 are packed in the tin. This will press the sides of the cases to the fondant as it sets, helping to achieve the traditional square shape of the fancies.

NB: Don't store the fancies in the fridge – it melts the fondant! Store them loosely covered in the cake tin or in a container, but not in a sealed plastic container as they will sweat. The syrup, marzipan, fondant and cupcake cases will enable them to stay fresh and moist for 2 or 3 days.

Blancmange for Nostalgic Adults and Poorly Children

Serves 10–15

300ml milk
Finely grated zest of ½ lemon
100g caster sugar
15g ground almonds
9 platinum gelatine leaves (see page 156)
850ml double cream
150g sweet seedless white grapes, halved,
    plus extra for decorating
Almond oil, for greasing

EQUIPMENT
Large decorative jelly mould
    (about 2-litre – I used a 2kg bundt
    mould)

*Variation: Leave out the grapes and once
the blancmange has set in the fridge, turn
it out and decorate it with a scattering of
pink crystallised rose petals.*

I've emphasised the slight 'hospital food' vibe of this dessert by adding sweet seedless white grapes to the top. These are authentic 'sultana' grapes from Turkey, and when you dry them, they do become, yes, sultanas! I found these white grapes at one of my favourite food shops, Where2Save, close to where I live. Corner shops, especially in cities with large immigrant populations, can have the freshest, cheapest and most interesting food. Obviously any seedless white grapes will do though.

Scald the milk in a small pan by heating it to just below boiling point. Remove from the heat, stir in the lemon zest, sugar and ground almonds, and leave to macerate for about an hour.

Soak the gelatine leaves in cold water, enough to sufficiently cover them, for a few minutes. When they are soft enough, squeeze out the water.

Bring the milk mixture to the boil in a pan, then strain it into a jug and add the gelatine, stirring until dissolved. Stir in the cream. Leave the mixture to cool to room temperature, stirring occasionally.

Oil your jelly mould with almond oil, then scatter the grapes into the base. Pour the cream mixture on top of the grapes. Leave to cool completely, then refrigerate for at least 2 hours or until set.

Carefully loosen and turn out the blancmange on to a serving plate (rinse the serving plate in cold water and leave it damp beforehand), then decorate with more grapes and serve.

Pastel Croquembouche

Makes 1 tower (serves about 20)

Double quantity of the Chouquettes
recipe on page 95

FOR THE CRÈME PÂTISSIÈRE
8 egg yolks
120g caster sugar
50g plain flour
50g cornflour
1 litre milk
1 vanilla pod, split in half lengthways and
seeds scraped out, or 1 tsp vanilla extract
A few drops of orange-blossom water

FOR THE GLACÉ ICING
250g icing sugar
A few drops of boiling water
3 food colouring pastes of your choice

FOR THE CARAMEL
300g caster sugar
300ml water

FOR DECORATION
Sugared almonds (I used silvered sugared
almonds, but pastel-coloured sugared
ones are fine too)
Crystallised violets or rose petals (optional)

EQUIPMENT
Piping bag fitted with a medium plain
nozzle
Sugar thermometer

This is the ultimate *pièce montée* and something I think every keen home baker should have a go at. Don't do it on a rainy or humid day or it will fall over and melt. Bake and fill your choux buns first, then construct the tower at the last minute. You can freestyle, piling them on top of one another in a pyramid, or buy a special mould covered with non-stick paper – you slide out the pyramid when you've finished constructing.

Usually croquembouche choux buns are dipped in caramel, but I think the flavour is boring with too much caramel. It's also rather hard on the teeth. I've made a very pretty pastel iced version. It still has spun sugar around it, which is another cookery skill that is well worth trying to make, as it is so impressive.

Make the choux buns (a double quantity) according to the Chouquettes recipe on page 95, but do not add the nibbed sugar at the end. Leave the cooked choux buns to cool completely.

Make the crème pâtissière by whisking together the egg yolks and caster sugar in a mixing bowl or stand mixer until light and fluffy. Add the two flours and mix until well combined. Set aside.

Bring the milk to the boil in a pan, then add the vanilla seeds or extract. Temper the custard by stirring one-third of the milk mix into the egg mix until combined, then return to the pan with the remaining milk mix and put it back on the hob. Bring gently to the boil, and when it starts to boil, turn down the heat and cook gently for a further 5 minutes. Add the orange-blossom water. Remove from the heat and leave to cool, then cover the pan with cling film and place it in the fridge to chill for 30 minutes.

Once the crème pâtissière is chilled enough to pipe, fill the piping bag with it. Puncture a hole in the bottom of each choux pastry bun and pipe in the crème.

To make the glacé icing, mix the icing sugar with a few drops of boiling water and whisk together until you have a shiny but not too liquid icing. Divide into three and mix each one with your chosen food colouring. Dip a third to a half of each choux bun into the glacé icing. Set aside to dry on a piece of parchment paper, icing-side up.

To make the caramel, first prepare a bowl of cold water large enough to take your pan. Put the caster sugar and water into a heavy-based pan and heat to 155°C (hard-crack stage). (Make sure you brush down the sides of the pan with water or leave the lid on until all of the sugar is melted.) Once the caramel is ready, remove the pan from the heat and carefully plunge the bottom of the pan into the bowl of cold water (making sure none splashes into the pan) to seize the temperature. If the caramel becomes too stiff you can re-heat it to the same temperature and go through the same process again.

How to Assemble Your Croquembouche

This is messy work so cover your table with parchment paper before you begin.

Assemble the croquembouche directly on your cake stand or serving plate. Using the caramel as a glue, stick the choux puffs together in circles on top of each other, working upwards in ever decreasing circles until they form a pyramid. Make sure the glacé icing is on the outside, alternating the colours. Stick the sugared almonds to the caramel at intervals and decorate with crystallised flowers, if using.

Hold two forks together, back to back, and dip them into the caramel. When you pull them out they will form a trail of spun sugar. Quickly trail the sugar all around the croquembouche. Serve immediately.

Champagne Rose Jellies

Makes 3–4 jellies

4 platinum gelatine leaves (see page 156),
   or 5g agar agar (see page 157)
400ml champagne
40g caster sugar
A few drops of rose water
4 organically grown or unsprayed fresh
   garden roses (flower heads) to fit your
   moulds

EQUIPMENT
3–4 jelly moulds (size depends on the size
   of your rose head but each about 100ml
   in volume) or pretty glasses (if not
   turning them out)

Ladies will flutter their fans and admire your elegant rose jellies. While roses are edible, ladies of a delicate disposition may wish to nibble around the edges of the jelly only. Eat with your eyes.

Soak the gelatine leaves in cold water, enough to sufficiently cover them, for a few minutes. When they are soft, squeeze out the water and put them into a heatproof bowl. Add a little champagne to cover, and microwave (on full power) for 10 seconds or so, or dissolve them gently in a bain-marie (see page 69). Once the gelatine has dissolved, add the sugar and rose water and the rest of the champagne and stir.

If using agar agar, put the champagne, sugar and rose water into a small pan and bring to the boil. Sprinkle over the agar agar and keep heating over a medium-high heat until the powder or flakes are dissolved, stirring all the time. The mixture is now ready to be poured into moulds.

If using rounded moulds, place some scrunched-up foil underneath each mould to keep it in place and secure. Place a rose in each mould (you want the bloom to show when the jelly is turned out) and pour over a little of the jelly mixture. Put the moulds in the fridge for an hour or so to set, then pour in the rest of the jelly, gently heating it up beforehand if it has started to set (it shouldn't do as jelly melts at room temperature). Put the jellies back in the fridge until completely set.

Serve the jellies only just before eating, as they will melt if kept at room temperature. If using agar agar, there is no need to chill the jellies as it keeps well at room temperature, but they will probably taste nicer if chilled. Carefully turn out each one on to a serving plate (or place the jellies in glasses on serving plates, if not using moulds) and serve.

Red & White Afternoon Tea

Inspired by the 'sweet stylist' Amy Atlas, many parties and weddings in the United States have 'sweet tables' or 'candy buffets'. Choose a colour or theme and match everything to it. It's visually stunning, and people can help themselves. This can also work for an afternoon tea.

STYLING TIPS:

Buy coloured balloons, paper pompoms, paper flags or bunting for overhead.

Coloured striped paper straws and baking cups with scalloped edges will look pretty on your table.

Buy ribbons and baking twine in the colours of your choice.

Look for old-fashioned glass sweetie jars at flea markets for your candies, or you can also buy them new.

Menu

Jam Sandwiches	*see page 33*
Sweet	
Stripy Meringue Kisses	*see opposite*
Ruby Shoe Biscuits	*see page 194*
Mini Cherry Bakewells	*see page 197*
Fleur de Sel Caramels	*see page 198*
Centrepiece	
Strawberry Heart Joconde Cake	*see page 199*
The Outrageous Multi–tiered Raspberry Pavlova	*see page 202*
Sweet Tree	*see page 204*
Drinks	
Russian Hot Jam 'Tea'	*see page 238*
Rose Petal Tea	*see page 233*
Hibiscus Tea	*see page 228*
Cherry Brandy	*see page 205*

Stripy Meringue Kisses

Makes 25–30

4 egg whites (weigh them – you want
   double the amount of sugar to egg whites)
240g caster sugar
½ tsp cream of tartar
A pinch of sea salt
Flavourings of your choice:
  – Here, I used a little rose water with
  red and purple striped meringue kisses
  but you could match the flavours
  to other colours of your choice, for
  instance, lemon essence with yellow
  striped meringue kisses. Or, peppermint
  extract and green stripes.
Food colouring paste in colours of your
  choice

EQUIPMENT
Several bowls for the different
  flavours/colours
Disposable piping bags,
  one for each flavour/colour
Thin paintbrush(es) (either rinse out the
  same paintbrush after using for each
  colour, or use a different paintbrush for
  each colour)

Take inspiration from The Meringue Girls from Hackney in London, and have a go at these toothpaste-striped meringues: frivolous, stylish, bite-sized and tasty! Sandwich them together in pairs with some whipped cream to make more substantial treats.

Preheat the oven to 110°C (gas ¼). Line 2 baking sheets with parchment paper or silicone mats.

In a scrupulously clean bowl, whisk the egg whites until they start to form soft peaks, then slowly add the sugar in a thin stream, whisking all the time. Add the cream of tartar and salt. Keep whisking until you have glossy stiff peaks. Divide the mixture into separate bowls (to make as many flavours as you wish) and stir a flavouring into each portion.

Stand a piping bag (one at a time) in a tall jug. Dip a paintbrush into a food colouring paste and paint a long stripe of food colouring from the inside of the bottom of the piping bag up to the top. Paint 2 or 3 stripes of your chosen food colouring in the piping bag in this way (leaving a space between each stripe). Then carefully scoop the meringue mixture into the bag, twist the top closed and cut off 5mm from the tip with scissors.

Holding the piping bag directly over your prepared baking sheets, pipe out 3cm mounds, flicking the piping tip off the ends to leave little peaks. You will see that the meringue mix comes out stripy, like toothpaste. It's very exciting. Space the mounds apart as they expand a little when cooked.

Repeat with the remaining flavoured meringue mixtures and food colouring pastes. You should be able to fit all the meringue kisses on the 2 baking sheets and the spacing apart should be sufficient to keep the colours separate.

Bake for 45–60 minutes. You know they are cooked when you can lift them off the baking sheet with the bottom intact. Leave to cool completely on the baking sheets.

You can serve these as they are, or you could sandwich them together in pairs with whipped cream or fruit curd, if you like.

Ruby Shoe Biscuits

Makes about 20

100g unsalted butter, softened
100g caster sugar
1 egg, lightly beaten
1 tsp vanilla extract
275g plain flour, plus extra for dusting

FOR THE ROYAL ICING
AND DECORATION
1 egg white
250g icing sugar
A squeeze of lemon juice
As much red food colouring paste as you
    need to give a deep colour
A small pot of edible red glitter

EQUIPMENT
Shoe-shaped cutter
Small sealable plastic containers
Small disposable piping bag
Pastry brush

For a *Wizard of Oz*-themed event, I made these Ruby Shoe Bis-cuits, covering the shoes with deep red icing and plenty of edible red glitter.

Preheat the oven to 180°C (gas 4). Line a baking sheet with parchment paper or a silicone mat.

Cream the butter and caster sugar together, then beat in the egg and vanilla extract. Stir in the flour until the mixture comes together as a dough.

Roll out the dough on a lightly floured work surface to 5mm thickness. Using your shoe-shaped cutter, cut out as many shoes as you can, rerolling the scraps. Place the shoe shapes on the prepared baking sheet.

Bake for 8–10 minutes or until springy to the touch. Leave the biscuits to firm up on the baking sheet for 5 minutes, then transfer to a wire rack and leave to cool completely.

To make the royal icing, put the egg white into a bowl, then add the icing sugar, stirring together until smooth and combined. Add a few drops of lemon juice and the red food colouring. Royal icing dries quickly, so immediately put the royal icing into several small airtight containers to prevent this.

Fill the piping bag with royal icing. Snip off a teeny bit of the end of the bag and pipe the icing around the edges of the biscuits, about a millimetre in from the edge. Add a little more lemon juice to the remaining royal icing, and make the tip of the bag slightly larger to 'flood' the inside of the biscuits. Fill the biscuits in with icing, wriggling the icing down the middle of each shoe and allowing it to spread.

Add the glitter decoration to the icing while it is still wet by dipping a dry pastry brush into the pot of glitter and flicking the brush over each iced shoe with your finger. You want an even layer of glitter.

Leave the biscuits to dry in a cool place for 24 hours before serving.

Mini Cherry Bakewells from The Secret Teapot

Makes 24

200g caster sugar
200g salted butter, softened
3 large eggs, beaten
150g self-raising flour, sifted
1 tsp baking powder
50g ground almonds
½ tsp almond extract
50g good-quality undyed glacé cherries,
    washed, dried and finely chopped

FOR THE ICING
Either glacé icing (made by combining
    250g icing sugar with a few drops of
    boiling water and stirring well until
    glossy)
- or -
1 quantity of Vanilla Buttercream Icing
    from the Cupcakes Baked in a Cup
    recipe (see page 106), replacing the
    vanilla extract with almond extract

12 pillar-box red glacé cherries, halved,
    to decorate
Icing sugar, for dusting (if using
    buttercream icing)

EQUIPMENT
24-hole mini muffin tray
24 paper mini muffin cases, red and white
    polka dot ones if possible
Piping bag fitted with a star-shaped nozzle
    (if topping with buttercream)

A Bakewell tart is iconically English, and covering it with glacé icing and decorating with a red cherry makes it look like a cheerful child's drawing of a cake. This is a guest recipe by Vicky Sponge of the Secret Teapot in Oxfordshire (see page 249), where Vicky serves these individual cherry Bakewells.

Preheat the oven to 180°C (gas 4). Line the muffin tray with paper muffin cases.

Place the caster sugar and butter in a large mixing bowl and beat together until light and fluffy. Gradually beat in the eggs, adding a spoonful of the sifted flour if the mixture looks like it is curdling. Fold in the rest of the flour and baking powder, then the ground almonds, almond extract and chopped cherries.

Divide the mixture evenly between the prepared muffin cases. You want roughly 15g of mixture in each case. You don't want them to rise too much or they will be difficult to ice.

Bake for 20 minutes or until a skewer inserted into the centre comes out clean. Cool in the tin for about 10 minutes, then transfer to a wire rack to cool completely.

If you want traditional tarts, top each baked cake with glacé icing and half a cherry.

Alternatively, if using buttercream icing, fill the piping bag with the buttercream. Starting at the outside of each cake, pipe a swirl of icing around the top of the cake and bring it to a point in the middle. Top each cake with half a cherry and dust with a little icing sugar just before serving.

Fleur de Sel Caramels

Makes 30

350ml double cream
400g caster sugar
250ml light corn syrup
 (see stockists on page 250)
55g unsalted butter, cubed
1 tsp vanilla extract
3 tsp sea salt

EQUIPMENT
Medium-deep 20cm square cake tin
Digital or sugar thermometer
Small wax paper squares, for wrapping

These are a bit scary to make (it seems to take ages for the caramel to heat up to the right temperature), but if you summon up
the courage, the results are very gratifying. When I served these
toffees wrapped in wax paper twists at an 18th-century-style
tea, they disappeared in minutes. I think people were stuffing
their pockets with them.

Line the cake tin with parchment paper (it should cover the bottom
and go up the sides slightly).

Place a medium heavy-based pan over a medium-low heat. Add
the cream, sugar and corn syrup and stir continuously with a wooden
spoon until it reaches 125°C (hard-ball stage), usually 20–30 minutes.

Remove the pan from the heat, then add the butter, vanilla extract and 2 teaspoons of the salt. Return to the heat and keep stirring
until the butter has melted. Remove from the heat, pour the mixture
into the prepared cake tin and then sprinkle with the last teaspoon
of salt.

Leave to cool and set, then cut into squares and wrap in small
wax paper squares. Store in an airtight container for up to 1 month.

Strawberry Heart Joconde Cake

Serves 10–12

FOR THE HEARTS
1 large egg white
30g granulated sugar
40g plain flour
20g unsalted butter, softened
Red or pink food colouring paste

FOR THE SPONGE
3 large egg whites
10g caster sugar
85g ground almonds
75g icing sugar, plus extra for dusting
25g plain flour
3 large eggs, beaten
30g unsalted butter, melted,
  plus extra for greasing

FOR THE BAVAROIS FILLING
12 platinum gelatine leaves (see page 156)
500ml milk
6 eggs
250g caster sugar
500g fresh strawberries, stalks removed
250g strawberry jam
750ml double cream
  (150ml of this will be used for topping
  the cake and piping the decoration)

EQUIPMENT
Piping bag fitted with a small plain nozzle
23cm springform cake tin
Piping bag fitted with a large star-shaped
  nozzle

This cake isn't as hard to make as it looks (see overleaf). I make it in a deep springform cake tin with a removable base. I've done a hearts design, but you can choose whatever joconde design you like: squiggly lines, polka dots, stripes or even writing.

First, prepare the template for the decorated sponge that will form the outside of your cake. You are going to bake a rectangle of sponge with which to line your cake tin, so measure the circumference and height of the tin and draw a rectangle on to a piece of parchment paper to fit those measurements. Flip over the paper so that the drawn template shows through and line a baking sheet with the paper. You will probably need to cut the template in half widthways and bake two rectangles (then join them together, end to end once they are baked), but they should both fit, side by side, on the same sheet (if not, prepare a second baking sheet, and place one on each sheet).

To make the hearts, in a small bowl, mix together the egg white, sugar, flour and butter until creamy. Add the food colouring until you have your desired shade. Scoop the mixture into the piping bag fitted with the plain nozzle and carefully pipe out your hearts on to the prepared baking sheet, within the rectangular template. This will form the pattern on the outside of your cake, so try to space the hearts evenly. I piped two rows of evenly-spaced hearts. Place the baking sheet in the freezer for 30 minutes or until the hearts are solid.

Meanwhile, make the sponge mixture. Whisk the egg whites and caster sugar together in a bowl until you have firm, glossy peaks. Sift the ground almonds, icing sugar and flour together in a separate bowl, then add the whole eggs, a little at a time, beating until well combined. Fold in a third of the whisked egg whites to lighten the batter, then fold in the remaining whisked egg whites until just combined. Add the melted butter and fold in until incorporated, then cover with cling film and set aside until the hearts pattern is set.

Preheat the oven to 200°C (gas 6).

Once your piped pattern is frozen solid, take it out of the freezer and use a spatula to gently spread the sponge batter over the top, within the rectangle template, to about 5mm thickness.

Bake for about 10 minutes or until springy to the touch, then leave to cool on the baking sheet for no longer than 5–10 minutes. While the sponge cools, dust a sheet of clean parchment paper (bigger than the cake you've baked) with icing sugar. Cut a separate length of parchment paper to fit around the inside of the spring-form ring and 1cm above the rim, then grease the inside edges of the tin and line with the parchment paper.

Invert the baked sponge on to the prepared sugar-dusted piece of paper. The cake will have spread during baking, so use a ruler or straight metal edge and a sharp knife to trim it back to the template, then peel off the parchment paper very carefully. You will now see your heart pattern in the rectangular sponge. Yay! Reserve the offcuts of sponge for the base.

Carefully line the inside edges of the tin with the rectangular heart-patterned sponge, with the pattern facing outwards. If you have made two rectangles, press the ends together. Cover the bottom of the tin with the offcuts of sponge, pieced together like a jig-saw (nobody will see the bottom) and press the edges together to seal them. Set aside.

Now, make the bavarois filling. Soak the gelatine leaves in cold water, enough to sufficiently cover them, for a few minutes. When they are soft, squeeze out the water. Meanwhile, gently bring the milk to the boil in a small pan. Remove from the heat.

In a bowl, whisk together the eggs and caster sugar until pale and thick. Temper the hot milk and eggs by pouring a little of the hot milk into the egg mixture, whisking, then pour in the rest of the hot milk. Whisk until thoroughly combined, then add the gelatine and whisk until dissolved.

Reserve 10–15 strawberries for decorating, then purée the rest in a blender or food processor. Add the strawberry purée to the egg mixture, along with the strawberry jam, and whisk to mix. In a separate bowl, whip 600ml of the cream until soft peaks form and then fold it into the strawberry mixture.

Carefully pour the bavarois mixture into the sponge-lined tin and then put the whole thing in the fridge for several hours to firm up.

About 10 minutes before you're ready to serve, whip the remaining cream to form firm peaks and spoon it into the piping bag fitted with a star-shaped nozzle.

Take the cake out of the fridge, unclip the tin, remove the cake tin and place the cake on a serving plate. Peel away the parchment paper. You should see your beautifully patterned heart-shaped sponge on the outside with the bavarois on the inside. Pipe rosettes of whipped cream around the top of the cake and pipe or spread a layer of cream over the top of the bavarois. Top with the reserved strawberries and serve with glasses of sweet champagne.

The Outrageous Multi-tiered Raspberry Pavlova

Serves 15

720g caster sugar
12 egg whites
2 tsp cream of tartar
A pinch of salt
1 jar (450g) seedless raspberry jam
    (optional)
900ml double cream
500g fresh raspberries
Icing sugar, for dusting

EQUIPMENT
2 large shallow baking tins
Large piping bag fitted with a large
    plain nozzle (or cut 1cm tip off a large
    disposable piping bag)

This can only be described as epic; here is my statuesque crimson and white lofty multi-storey pav.

Preheat the oven to 200°C (gas 6). Line both baking tins with parchment paper or silicone mats.

As this is such a large meringue with a risk of sugar weepage, let's do the Ottolenghi method of making big meringues. We are going to warm up the caster sugar so that there are no undissolved crystals in the meringue mix. Pour the caster sugar evenly into the prepared baking tins, splitting it into two. Heat the sugar in the oven for about 8 minutes, until the edges start to brown slightly. Remove from the oven.

Turn the oven down to 110°C (gas ¼). Line 2 baking sheets with parchment paper or silicone mats.

Meanwhile, pour the egg whites into your stand mixer or a large bowl and start to whisk until they become thick, then gradually whisk in the warm caster sugar, followed by the cream of tartar and the pinch of salt. Keep whisking until you have stiff peaks.

Prop the piping bag in a jug and pour the meringue mixture into it. Pipe the base of your pavlova on to one of the prepared baking sheets by piping out a circle of 9 swirly mounds that are touching at the edges (each swirly mound should be about 6cm in diameter and 5cm high). Fill in the middle of the circle with more meringue.

Then, on the second prepared baking sheet, pipe the middle and top tiers. You will need 5 swirly mounds (again, each about 6 x 5cm) for the middle tier, filled with meringue, and 1 large swirly mound, about 8 x 5cm, for the top.

Bake the bottom tier for 3 hours and the middle and top tiers for 2 hours, until they are hard on top and they appear to be dry and lift easily off the parchment paper with the bottom intact.

If you like (and this is optional), when the meringue is almost cooked, gently heat up the jam in a small pan until it is liquid, and then remove from the heat. Then, pulling the baking sheets out of the oven, use a spoon to swirl some of this jam on top of each meringue layer. Return the meringues to the oven until cooked.

Remove from the oven. Leave the meringues to cool completely on the baking sheets, then carefully remove the largest/bottom layer and place on a large platter.

Whip the cream in a bowl to form stiff peaks and then spoon about half on to the base layer of meringue. Carefully place the middle meringue layer on top and spoon the remaining whipped cream on top. Place the final meringue layer on top of the pavlova, stud all over with the raspberries and sift icing sugar over the top. Serve immediately.

Sweet Tree

Makes 1

*Sweets of your choice; for this I used red
marshmallow sweets, but use any
sweets you can stick a cocktail stick into*
*Small sweets for the pot; I used small
white and pink tic tacs, but use anything
you like*

EQUIPMENT
Small bag (500g) plaster of Paris
*Small plant pot (plastic or terracotta both
ok to use) or small tin, any holes sealed*
*Wooden baton, cut to the height that will
fit your plant pot without toppling over*
*Round ball of florist's oasis (use one that
is the same size/diameter as the pot or
slightly larger than the pot)*
Tissue paper (white or coloured)
Pretty twine or ribbon
Cocktail sticks

These are very popular at the moment, a bauble of sweeties in
the manner of topiary, ideal for a centrepiece. They are very easy
and cheap to make yourself! I found the equipment at Hobbycraft
(see stockists on page 250) or on eBay.

Mix the plaster of Paris according to the packet instructions, then
pour it into your plant pot or tin to three-quarters full. Quickly place
the wooden baton vertically in the centre, about 4 or 5cm down, and
hold it in place until the plaster has dried around it.

Once the baton is secure, plunge the ball of oasis on to the ex-
posed end, but not so far that the baton comes out of the top. You
want it about three-quarters of the way through the oasis. Cover the
oasis with tissue paper and secure around the bottom, where it meets
the wooden baton, with pretty twine or ribbon tied in a bow.

Plunge the cocktail sticks into your sweets and then stick them
all around the oasis ball. Hide the top surface of the pot with more
tissue paper and cover with smaller sweets.

Cherry Brandy

Makes 1 bottle (1 litre)

500g fresh cherries, stalks intact
250g caster sugar
1 bottle (70cl) vodka

EQUIPMENT
1.5-litre sterilised jar (see page 41)
1-litre sterilised bottle (see page 41), or you could
use 2 x 500ml bottles or other pretty bottles
(sterilised, of course) and give this as a gift

Do you remember those wonderful cherry liqueur chocolates 'Mon Chéri' packaged in their characteristic Valentine-red box? I used to ask for them in my Christmas stocking every year. This is like a bottle of the stuff inside the chocolate: rich, sweet and slightly bitter from the cherry stones.

Rinse the cherries but leave about a centimetre of stalk on each one. Retaining the stalks means the cherries will remain firm. Layer the cherries with the sugar in the sterilised jar and pour over the alcohol. Seal the jar, then leave in a dark cupboard at room temperature and turn every day for a week; this is a recipe that only gets better and stronger, the longer you leave it.

Once it is ready, strain the alcohol from the fruit (the cherries can be used in desserts, such as clafoutis and strudels, or as a topping for ice cream). Using a funnel, pour the alcohol into a pretty sterilised bottle or two and seal. If you're planning to give them as gifts, add a label and some pretty ribbon to each bottle. Cherry brandy will keep for a year or so in a cool, dark, dry place.

Oriental-themed Afternoon Tea

ea originally came from China, and it is an integral part of life there. Japan and China both have ritual tea ceremonies. Indulge in some oriental flavours for this party.

STYLING TIPS FOR THE TABLE:

·········· Use a china tea set with tiny, delicate cups. ··········
·········· Use cherry blossom sprigs as table decorations. ··········
·········· Provide chopsticks and serve good-quality Chinese tea. ··········
·········· Play chiming music in the background. ··········
·········· Have Chinese lanterns glowing around the room. ··········

STYLING TIPS FOR THE HOSTESS AND GUESTS:

·········· Wear a kimono or cheongsam dress. ··········
·········· Give your guests Chinese shawls and fans. ··········

Menu

Savoury

Banh Mi	*see opposite*
Tamagoyaki Rolled Omelette Sushi	*see page 208*
Matcha Scones	*see page 46*

Sweet

Tea etiquette: tapping the table means you'd like a refill. As is taking off the teapot lid and leaving it at an angle on top of the pot. The lid of the teapot should never be left on the table, this allows good luck to escape.

Taiyaki Cakes	*see page 210*
Fortune Cookies	*see page 212*
Lavender Temari Cakes	*see page 214*
Pandan Custard Tarts	*see page 218*

Drinks

Bubble Tea	*see page 219*
Cherry Blossom Tea	*see page 230*

Banh Mi

Serves 4

Fresh baguettes (either one large or 4 small)
Unsalted butter, at room temperature
Mayonnaise
Sriracha chilli sauce
Cucumber, thinly sliced
Spring onions, thinly sliced
1 fresh red or green chilli, deseeded and
   thinly sliced
Fresh coriander sprigs
Lime juice
Sea salt

FOR THE PICKLES
4–5 carrots, grated
1 daikon (white radish), grated
300ml rice vinegar
150ml water
100g caster sugar
25g sea salt

FOR THE MUSHROOM PÂTÉ
3 tbsp rapeseed oil
1 tbsp sesame oil
1 shallot, diced
300g button mushrooms, sliced
2 tbsp soy sauce
2 tbsp five-spice powder
Freshly ground black pepper, to taste

EQUIPMENT
1-litre sterilised jar (see page 41)

This is a very tasty vegetarian version of the traditional Viet-namese sandwiches, which uses mushroom pâté instead of the meat pâté.

First, make the pickles. Put the grated carrots and daikon into the sterilised jar. In a pan, gently heat the vinegar, water, sugar and salt together, stirring and heating just until the sugar and salt have dis-solved. Remove from the heat, pour into the jar over the vegetables, seal, cool and then refrigerate for at least 2 hours or overnight.

To make the mushroom pâté, heat the oils in a frying pan over a medium heat. Add the shallot and fry gently until soft. Add the mushrooms, soy sauce and five-spice powder and fry until cooked, about 5–10 minutes. Season with black pepper, then remove from the heat, transfer to a blender and blend to a fine pâté consistency.

Split your baguette(s) open and butter one side. Spread the mush-room pâté on top of the butter. Spread the mayonnaise and chilli sauce on the other side. Then add the cucumber, spring onions, chilli and coriander, placing them all along the baguette(s). Top with some of the drained pickles. Add a squeeze of lime juice and season with salt. Cut into diagonal wedges to serve.

Tamagoyaki Rolled Omelette Sushi

Serves 1–2

Knob of unsalted butter, for frying
3 stems of broccoli or sprouting broccoli
    (choose the slimmest)
A little boiling water, for braising
2 eggs
1 tbsp caster sugar
A pinch of sea salt
1 tbsp cold water
1 tbsp soy/tamari/shoyu sauce,
    or ponzu sauce
A little vegetable oil, for frying
Soy sauce, to serve

EQUIPMENT
A medium-sized decent frying pan; if you
    have a rectangular one, all the better

This is a recipe for broccoli that can be done in 10 minutes. It's called tamagoyaki in Japan and, to be authentic, should be cooked in a rectangular frying pan.

The omelette is very thin because the egg is diluted with a little water. It also requires some serious chopstick nimbleness. I'm not gonna lie, it's harder than it looks. Do your best, it'll taste great anyway.

I came up with this healthy, low fat, very quick Japanese omelette roll recipe. Low fat, I say? Very unlike me. Use any fine stems of broccoli or sprouting broccoli. Or use asparagus.

Melt the knob of butter in the frying pan over a medium heat. Place the broccoli in the pan and then add a little boiling water, just enough to cover the stems. Braise for 4 minutes, until the stems are tender. Drain the broccoli and set it aside. Wipe the moisture from the pan.

In a bowl, whisk together the eggs, sugar, salt, cold water and sauce. Heat a little vegetable oil in your frying pan, just enough to cover the bottom, and then pour in the egg mixture so that it covers the bottom of the pan.

Once the egg begins to set, return the broccoli stems to the pan, laying them next to each other over the omelette, stem to tip. Using a spatula, roll the omelette over the stems. You are aiming for a rolled Japanese-style omelette with the bright green crisp broccoli stems inside.

Serve whole or sliced crossways, with a small dipping bowl of soy sauce on the side.

Taiyaki Cakes

Makes 6

60ml milk, warmed
2 eggs, beaten
50g caster sugar
100g plain flour
½ tsp baking powder
¾ tsp sea salt
Small tin (250g) sweet chestnut purée
   (this will be enough for double or
   even triple this recipe)
Unsalted butter, for greasing

EQUIPMENT
Taiyaki pan (see stockists on page 250)

Options: Try filling your fish with chopped chocolate (dark or milk chocolate works best) or crème pâtissière (see page 188) instead of the chestnut purée.

Taiyaki cakes are fish-shaped pancakes, usually filled with sweet bean paste, that are popular as a street food in Korea and Japan. I bought a taiyaki pan on eBay that cost about £20 with shipping.

I'm not a huge fan of sweet bean paste, and it occurred to me that sweet chestnut purée, not dissimilar in texture and taste, is more palatable for European tastes, and could be a replacement. It worked very well – so well that I've left a plate in the hallway for the residents of the other flats in my house. I don't have the teen as a guinea pig anymore and I can't eat them all, so it's nice to share, isn't it?

These can be heated up, wrapped in foil in a low oven, or unwrapped briefly in the microwave (on full power), if you don't want to eat them straight away.

Pour the warm milk into a bowl, add the eggs and mix together. Add the rest of the ingredients, except the sweet chestnut purée and the butter for greasing, and whisk together until combined to make a batter.

Grease your taiyaki pan with butter and stand it on the hob over a medium heat, making sure the deeper side is on the bottom and the shallower side is on the top.

Pour enough of the batter into the deep side of the pan, to thinly cover the entire mould. Add some chestnut purée (I put a dollop in the middle and then a little more for the tail). Add some more batter on top to cover the chestnut purée. Leave for 1 minute, then turn the pan over, clamping both sides together firmly, and cook for 30 seconds more.

Remove the pan from the heat. Using a sharp knife, cut away any excess batter, retaining the shape of the fish, and then ease it out of the pan on to a serving plate. Keep warm while you cook the remaining taiyaki cakes in the same way, then serve.

Eat! Maybe served with some green tea?

Fortune Cookies

Makes 16

2 large egg whites
1 tsp orange-blossom water
2 tbsp vegetable oil
1 tbsp sesame oil
80g plain flour
1½ tsp cornflour
¼ tsp sea salt
120g caster sugar
3 tsp water

Millions of fortune cookies or *tuiles* are manufactured every day. Originally the messages were Chinese sayings, some of which were poorly translated and made no sense. Nowadays, fortune cookie factories employ writers. The cookies often contain lottery numbers, which are generated by a computer. In March 2005, US lottery officials suspected a scam when 110 people claimed the prize of $100,000 as opposed to the usual handful. When they investigated it, they discovered the sequence of digits came from a fortune cookie!

For your oriental tea, why not devise your own personalised fortunes? The pieces of paper should measure about 6 x 1cm. Here are some examples: 'May you live in interesting times' (for those of you that don't know, this is a Chinese curse!); or 'You will be hungry again in 1 hour'.

Preheat the oven to 170°C (gas 3). Line a baking sheet with parchment paper or a silicone mat. Make your fortunes.

Beat the egg whites, orange-blossom water and oils together in a bowl until frothy. Sift the flour, cornflour, salt and sugar into another bowl. Add the water to the flour mixture. Add the egg mixture to the flour mix and stir until you have a smooth batter.

Bake these cookies in three batches of 5 or 6 at a time. Place tablespoons of the batter on to the prepared baking sheet and then use the back of a metal spoon to swirl out the mixture into 10cm circles. Leave space between each cookie as they will spread a little during cooking.

Bake for 10–12 minutes, until light golden brown, then remove from the oven. Remove each cookie from the baking sheet with a spatula and place a rolled-up fortune in the centre of each one. Very quickly, while the cookie is still soft and pliable, fold it in half and pinch the edges together to seal. Place the folded edge of the cookie over the rim of a cup and gently pull the two corners down, to form the classic fortune cookie shape. Transfer to a wire rack to cool.

Repeat with the remaining batter until all your fortune cookies are baked and shaped. Store in an air-tight container. If the cookies have softened by the time you come to serve them, crisp them up in the oven for a few minutes.

Lavender Temari Cakes

Makes 3 sphere cakes (6 halves);
each sphere cake serves 3–4 people

115g unsalted butter, softened, plus extra for greasing
115g caster sugar
Finely grated zest of ½ lemon
3 drops of culinary lavender oil, or 1 tbsp culinary dried
    lavender (see stockists on page 250)
115g eggs, or 2 eggs, lightly beaten
115g plain flour, plus extra for dusting
5g or 1 slightly heaped tsp baking powder
A pinch of sea salt

FOR THE LAVENDER AND LEMON SYRUP
75g caster sugar
75ml water
A drop of culinary lavender oil,
    or 1 tsp culinary dried lavender
Juice of 1 lemon

FOR THE BUTTERCREAM
75g unsalted butter, softened
225g icing sugar, plus extra for dusting
1–2 drops of culinary lavender oil,
    or finely grated zest of ½ lemon
2 tsp milk

FOR THE FILLING
3 tbsp shop-bought or home-made Lemon Curd (see page 122)
    or 3 tbsp lemon marmalade with lavender (see stockists
    on page 250)
Another option, adding a teaspoon of Nutella
    (for Home-made 'Nutella', see page 45)

TO DECORATE
2 x 454g packs marzipan (yellow or white, the choice is yours)
    (you will have some left over)
2 x 500g packs fondant/sugar paste icing
    (you will have some left over)
Food colouring paste of your choice (optional)
Boiled water, left to cool
1 quantity of Royal Icing (see page 71)
Edible white disco hologram glitter

EQUIPMENT
1 silicone cake mould with 6 half sphere indentations –
    each half sphere indentation is about 85ml (often sold as
    chocolate tea cake moulds) (see stockists on page 250)
Pastry brush
Palette knife
Rolling pin
Piping bag fitted with a small plain nozzle

Working with my friend Michelle Eshkeri of The Lavender Bakery (see page 184) we developed our own version of Japanese baker Maki's temari cakes (see page 251).

The lemon and lavender cake is Michelle's signature cake, and these two flavours combine exquisitely. This recipe is easier than it might appear. Take it stage by stage, and you'll be so proud of your temari cakes.

It is really worth buying the culinary lavender oil (see stockists on page 250) for these cakes. It lasts a long time and can be used in many recipes both sweet and savoury. It is especially good in short-bread and ice cream. Another option to infuse lavender flavour into baked goods is to make some lavender sugar with dried organic lavender. Place a few tablespoons of dried lavender in a jar with some caster sugar, cover and leave in a cupboard for a week or two. Sift the dried flowers out before using the infused sugar for baking.

The sharpness of the lemon provides a good balance to the sweetness of the cake and its coverings; it both complements and tempers the lavender flavour. It is best to make the cakes a day in advance so that they're not too fragile to work with.

Preheat the oven to 180°C (gas 4). Lightly grease the cake mould with butter, then dust with flour and tip out the excess.

Place the butter, caster sugar, lemon zest and lavender oil or dried lavender in a bowl. Using an electric hand-held whisk, cream together for 8–10 minutes or until very pale and fluffy, scraping down the sides of the bowl occasionally with a rubber spatula. Gradually beat in the eggs, making sure each amount is fully incorporated before the next addition. Fold in the sifted flour, baking powder and salt.

Place the silicone mould on your kitchen scales (on a tray if necessary) and weigh 75g of mix into each indentation. They should each be about three-quarters full. Smooth the mixture flat and then place the mould on a baking sheet. Bake for 15–20 minutes or until the cakes spring back when lightly pressed with a finger. Don't open the oven door for the first 15 minutes or they might collapse, and don't worry if the mixture spreads over the top of the moulds a little, as the excess will be sliced off when they are cooled. Leave the cakes to cool in the moulds for 10 minutes, then carefully turn out on to a wire rack and leave to cool completely.

When you are ready to assemble the cakes, make the lavender and lemon syrup by combining the sugar and water in a small pan over a low heat and stirring until the sugar has dissolved. Increase the heat to medium-high and cook until the syrup comes to the boil. Remove from the heat and pour into a bowl; leave to cool. Add the lavender oil, if using, and the lemon juice to the cool syrup. If you are using the dried lavender rather than the oil, then pour the hot syrup on to the dried flowers to infuse while it cools, then strain before use and stir in the lemon juice. Set aside.

Make the buttercream by beating together the butter, icing sugar and lavender oil or lemon zest in a bowl with an electric hand-held whisk. Beat for at least 5 minutes, gradually adding the milk if the mixture seems too stiff – the buttercream needs to have a fairly soft consistency for covering the spheres.

Slice any excess cake off the flat sides of the sponges with a serrated knife, so you have 6 perfect half spheres. Hollow out a tablespoon of sponge from the centre of the flat side of each one and, using a teaspoon, fill with some buttercream and the lemon curd or marmalade. Don't overfill – the half spheres need to easily fit together and remain spherical rather than egg-shaped! Use a little more buttercream as glue to attach 2 half spheres together. You should now have 3 round/sphere cakes in front of you.

Slice a small sliver off the bottom of each sphere so that they sit flat. This will make it easier to decorate them. Brush all over the cakes with the lavender and lemon syrup using a pastry brush. It is best to soak them with as much syrup as possible without them becoming soggy, as this keeps the cakes moist as well as providing an extra layer of texture and flavour.

Give the cakes a few minutes to absorb the syrup and then use a palette knife to spread a layer of buttercream over each sphere. Cover them completely but don't worry if it isn't smooth. Place each cake on a small cake board or plate and cover with a piece of cling film. Use your hands to smooth the covered cakes all over – the cling film allows this to be done without a huge amount of mess and also makes it possible to ensure a smooth and round shape to the cakes that will be a good base for the marzipan and fondant coverings.

Leave the cling film on the cakes and place them in the fridge for several hours or until cold and set.

To decorate, for the marzipan layer, knead the marzipan a little until it is softened. Divide into 3 equal pieces, then cover 2 pieces with cling film while you work with the first. Sprinkle icing sugar on the work surface and the rolling pin, then roll out the marzipan to 3mm thickness. Using a sharp knife, cut out a circle that is a little bigger than you think you will need to completely cover one of the sphere cakes. Remove a cake from the fridge and peel off the cling film. Drape the marzipan circle over the buttercream-coated cake. Mould the marzipan gently over the sphere so it is completely covered; smoothing from the top down with your hands so that it doesn't tear and so you don't get pleats, which will make it lumpy. Trim off any excess with a knife and fill any holes with small pieces of marzipan. Smooth all over with your hands to keep the round shape but don't over handle it – you don't want to melt the buttercream or lose the sphere shape, so work quickly and lightly. Repeat with the remaining marzipan and sphere cakes. Leave to dry somewhere dark and cool overnight.

The next day, knead the fondant icing a little to soften it and then work in some food colouring, if you like. Divide into 3 equal pieces, then cover 2 pieces with cling film while you work with the first. Have cooled boiled water and a pastry brush ready. Lightly dust your work surface with icing sugar. Again, work with one cake at a time; roll out the first piece of fondant icing to 3mm thickness and then cut out a rough circle that is a little bigger than you need to completely cover a marzipan-covered sphere cake. Brush the marzipan lightly with the water, then drape the rolled fondant icing over the top. Mould and smooth the icing in the same way that you did with the marzipan. Repeat with the remaining fondant icing and marzipan-covered sphere cakes.

Place each sphere cake on a separate serving plate. Decorate with royal icing piped using a small plain nozzle in small star-like stripes or in a looping pattern starting in the middle at the top of the cake, and finally sprinkle with hologram glitter before serving.

Pandan Custard Tarts

Asians love afternoon tea and cake, and pandan is the Asian version of vanilla. It has a subtle flavour that works well in sweet dishes.

You can buy pandan leaves from any Asian supermarket. Simply follow the recipe for Portuguese Custard Tarts on page 102, but knot 2–3 pandan leaves and infuse the milk and cream before making up the custard. Even easier, buy pandan essence from Asian supermarkets or online (see stockists on page 250). If you like the taste, you can mix the custard with cream and freeze it to make ice cream!

Or, you can make your own pandan essence. Buy 15–20 pandan leaves (they are sold in bunches in Asian supermarkets; you can keep any leftovers in the freezer) and blitz them in a blender with 100ml water. Strain into a bowl, then cover and keep the mixture in the fridge for 2 days. The mixture will separate, and the darker, bottom part is the pandan essence. Simply tip the top part away and discard; the essence you are left with will then keep for up to a week in the fridge.

Bubble Tea

Makes 2 jars (serves 2)

100g dried white, black or multicoloured
  tapioca pearls
4 tbsp caster sugar
About 500ml boiling water for the tea,
  plus extra for cooking the tapioca pearls
2 black tea bags
Ice cubes
Sweetened condensed milk, to taste

EQUIPMENT
2 jars with lids
  (I recommend jars because they have lids and you
  can shake the tea; I used 500ml Kilner jars – see
  stockists on page 250)
Wide drinking straws (see stockists on page 250)

This is the classic bubble tea recipe.

Put the tapioca pearls and sugar into a pan with enough boiling water to cover and cook for about 15 minutes; when they float, they are cooked. Turn off the heat and leave the pearls to sit in the water for another 15 minutes, then drain.

Make 2 large cups (about 500ml, depending on the size of your cups or jars) of strong black tea using the tea bags and the remaining boiling water.

Remove and discard the tea bags, then pour the tea into the two jars and add half of the cooked tapioca pearls to each jar. Top up each one with ice cubes and add condensed milk to taste. Put the lids on the jars and shake them up.

Serve the bubble tea in the jars with wide drinking straws (remove the lids just before serving).

5. Liquid Wisdom

'A woman is like a tea bag. You don't know
how strong she is until she is in hot water.'
Eleanor Roosevelt

'I would rather have a cup of tea than sex.'
Boy George

Proper Tea

Tea is the world's second most consumed beverage after water. Good tea can be very expensive. Some batches are sought after by investors and teaophiles and can cost more than premier cru Bordeaux wines.

The most expensive cup of tea I've ever had cost £15 for a (quite tiny) cup in a fashionable teahouse in Spitalfields, east London. I can't honestly say that I felt it was worth the money but clearly my palate needs educating, there is much to learn about tea.

While tea as a drink is soothing, politically, it causes trouble. For instance, you could argue that the reason the UK lost its American colonies was down to tea. Our attempts to tax tea led to the Boston Tea Party, where ships were boarded by angry rebels and tea crates were dumped into Boston harbour. No wonder America mostly drinks coffee. (George Washington drank hot chocolate.)

In the 19th century, tea drinking in the UK was encouraged, especially for the middle and working classes, as an antidote to drinking alcohol. Prior to tea, everybody drank beer, including children. Samuel Johnson, for instance, was addicted to all types of tea, at a time when the leaves cost so much they were locked up in a lead-lined tea caddy. Tea still represents revolt against the establishment in America: right-winger Sarah Palin was a leader of the Tea Party, an acronym for Taxed Enough Already.

Real tea is whole leaf rather than the shavings that we find in our average tea bag. We forget, even, that tea is leaves. All tea, be it white, green or black, comes from the same bush, *Camellia Sinensis*. The difference lies in how it is processed.

In my childhood, we didn't use tea bags, we used a teapot and a strainer. In 1968, only 3 per cent of the population used tea bags. Today only 3 per cent use leaf tea. If you are going to the effort of a proper afternoon tea, it is worth dusting off your best teapots and using loose leaf tea. This also saves time and tea, for you can brew enough for several people in one go.

In Britain most of us use electric kettles to boil the water for our tea. Electricity usage shoots upwards dramatically after episodes of popular TV programmes like *Eastenders* have just finished, when 1.75 million electric kettles are switched on simultaneously. The UK is obliged to borrow electricity from the French to cover the energy spikes. No other country experiences power surges in the same way, such is our dependence on tea as national succour, calmant, restorative.

George Orwell, in between predicting a dystopian future in *1984* and sleeping rough in London and Paris, wrote an essay on the importance of tea. He insisted on ceramic teapots, tall mugs, no creamy milk (added afterwards), extremely strong tea and no sugar.

Henrietta Lovell, the Rare Tea Lady (you may have seen her on *The Apprentice*), who travels all over the world discovering the very best tea, gives the following advice:

- Warm the pot with a cup of boiling water, then tip it out. This will raise the temperature of the pot and keep the tea warmer for longer.
- Allow one teaspoon of tea and a cup of water for each person. The adage 'one for the pot', an extra teaspoon for the pot, applies only if you like very strong tea.
- Water temperature: for industrial tea, yes, you need the standard boiling water, but for more delicate, posher teas, you need a temperature of, on average, 85°C. But, without getting too geeky, every category of tea requires a certain ideal water temperature. Most of us use an electric kettle to boil water so I did a temperature test: how hot is electric-kettle-boiled water? It turns out my kettle is just under the official boiling temperature of 100°C, at more like 92–95°C. I then poured out the water and timed it until it got to 85°C: it took a full minute. I then added the tea.
- Loose leaf teas take longer to brew than tea bags. Three minutes is about right, depending on your preferred strength.
- Don't leave the tea to steep once it is brewed, strain it out.
- Putting the correct amount of boiling water in the pot means that you can drain and refill it a second or third time using the same tea leaves, if you are using good-quality tea. The Chinese believe the third brewing to be the most flavoursome.

Optimum Water Temperatures for Tea

Tea	Water Temperature	Steep Time
Green	70–85°C (air bubbles start to rise)	1–3 mins
White	76–85°C (air bubbles are rising fairly fast)	2–8 mins and up to 15 mins
Black	85–95°C	1–3 mins
Oolong	95–100°C	1–4 mins
Herbal tisanes	100°C (full boil)	3–10 mins
Blooming (Black)	85–95°C	3–10 mins
Blooming (Green)	70–85°C (air bubbles start to rise)	3–10 mins

Builder's Tea

Boiling water
Milk
Sugar
Tea

EQUIPMENT
Kettle, teapot
Milk jug, sugar basin
Tea tray (optional)
Cups, saucers and teaspoons

Traditionally builder's tea is made with an Assam blend and served in a sturdy mug. If you want a builder to turn up, stay on the job and work hard, make sure you serve this type of tea at regular intervals throughout the day.

I like weak tea without too much tannin, with milk, and without sugar. I call it pissy Southern tea. My daughter started university in York and has come back as a northerner, a Stark of Winterfell, for she now drinks deep tan tea with sugar. I'm thinking of disowning her.

Whatever your tipple, every afternoon tea should offer a standard builder's–type tea in addition to more exotic ones. My recipe? You want a recipe for a cup of tea, which every person from the British Isles should know? All right, I will give you the 'recipe' from my very first cookbook, Good Housekeeping's *Children's Cook Book*.

Put a kettle of fresh water to heat. (This was pre-electric kettles and pre-tea bags.) When it boils, pour a little into the teapot and leave it to warm.

Meanwhile, pour the milk into the jug, put sugar into a basin and get a tea tray ready, if required, laying out the cups and saucers.

Throw away the water from the pot; add tea, allowing 1 heaped teaspoon per person and 1 extra for the pot.

Pour on really boiling water, three-quarters filling the pot. Leave for 2 minutes before pouring out the tea.

Note: No judgements about sugar in tea, despite George Orwell's injunction against it.

Milk

The British originally added milk and sugar to tea to allay bitterness. Milk can go in before or after the tea, although your choice inevitably has class ramifications – Nancy Mitford, Evelyn Waugh and George Orwell all agreed that milk-in-first was the middle-, rather than the upper-class method. It's true that adding milk afterwards means you can accurately judge the colour and strength of your tea, however, chemist Dr Stapley of Loughborough University says that adding cold milk to hot tea causes the milk proteins to clump. In the UK we use pasteurised fresh milk, which is why tea never tastes the same abroad, a horrible experience that starts on the ferry to France, where they tend to have boiled (UHT) milk in mini plastic pods. You can use milk in all black teas.

Condensed milk is amazing in tea. See the Masala Chai recipe on page 227.

Tea Bags

American tea dealer Thomas Sullivan invented tea bags in 1904, when he realised it was more economical to send out samples in silk bags rather than tins. Tea bags came over to the UK in the late 1960s. Now most tea is brewed in bags.

My favourite tea bag tea is Barry's tea from Ireland. It has a wonderful caramel colour without the need to steep it too long, and a lingering, refreshing taste. It's not easy to get in British supermarkets, although I know I can stock up if I visit Neal's Yard Dairy in Borough Market, London. Failing that, Yorkshire Tea is pretty good.

You can blend and fill your own tea bags, a cute idea. See details of a workshop on page 233.

Loose Leaf Tea

Most types of tea are still sold loose as well as in bags, but quality varies from small chips of sawdust to rolled leaves beautifully unfurling in hot water. The array of teas (there are about 5000 varieties) could take a lifetime to explore. Let me give you a very brief primer:

Black Tea

The most expensive tea in the world is a rare Chinese tea called Tieguanyin, which is priced at £1,700 per kilo, or £130 per cup. It is fertilised by Panda dung. 'Da Hong Pao', which derives from three original tea bushes planted on Mount Wuyi in China about a thousand years ago, also claims to be the most expensive.

Within the overall category of black teas we have different types including:

Darjeeling: very floral and perfumed. Can be drunk without milk.
Lapsang Souchong: a smoked tea. Can be drunk without milk.
Assam: the base for English breakfast tea. Strong, malty.
Ceylon: strong, almost spicy. The base for many Earl Grey teas.
Earl Grey: perfumed and flavoured with bergamot citrus oil. Can be drunk without milk.
Lady Grey: Earl Grey and cornflowers.

Oolong

Oolong tea is partly oxidised, another word for aged or fermented. The three sacred tea bushes on Mount Wuyi are oolongs. Drink enough high-quality oolong and you can get 'drunk' on it: either you get the shakes or you feel mildly euphoric.

Green Tea

Green tea is differentiated from black tea by the fact that it is not oxidised. It is treated with heat rapidly after picking to preserve the fresh green flavour; same plant, different process. There are two methods for heat-treating green tea: dry and steam. The dry stuff is called Long Jing, or Gunpowder tea, and can be very expensive. The steamed green tea 'Sencha' comes from Japan, and is also the origin of Matcha, a powdered green tea. This type of processing gives a grassier, more vegetal flavour.

Some people find green tea very bitter, but it's important to buy a good brand of high-quality green tea, to not use boiling water and to not steep it for too long. Green tea has many health qualities. Drink it without sugar or milk. Milk turns it grey.

Red Tea

Rooibos isn't actually tea (it comes from a different plant) but it's one of my favourite drinks and contains no caffeine. (Tea has about 40mg less caffeine per cup than with coffee.) It's also very low in tannin so you can stew it for as long as you like. It is a speciality of South Africa, and attempts to grow it elsewhere have failed. Rooibos is a flavoursome, healthy alternative to caffeinated tea.

Pu-erh Tea

Pu-erh is fermented or oxidised tea. It's sold in compressed 'cakes', the best coming from wild trees. It is chocolatey, smoky and dark.

Pulled Tea

This *chai*-style tea, a speciality of Malaysia and Singapore, is poured rapidly from one cup, or jug, into another, with a stream of milky, tan-coloured liquid going from one to the other, looking like a rope. This 'pulling' technique cools the tea, improves its flavour, introduces air, and leaves a froth on top. It's a sort of *chai* cappuccino. I would advise looking at a few YouTube videos to see how it's done before embarking on it yourself. It is, however, very spectacular. Frothy tea seems to be a particularly Asian ambition. They even produce bamboo whisks in China for this very purpose.

Tea Ceremony

In Japan, tea drinking can require beating on a gong five times in a ceremony that can last several hours. It's rather like a British afternoon tea party in terms of length and formality, although we tend to leave out the gong.

Masala Chai

Makes 2–3 cups

500ml boiling water
1 tbsp loose black tea leaves
    or 1–2 bags of black Indian tea
75ml condensed milk
1–2 tsp palm sugar/jaggery

FOR THE CHAI MASALA SPICE MIX
10 black peppercorns
1 tsp ground ginger
1 cinnamon stick
5 green cardamom pods, split
4 whole cloves
1 tbsp ground nutmeg

Tea in China and India is called *chai* or *cha*. The old phrase 'a cup of char' stems from this other word for tea. Travelling in India, you hear the singsong call 'chaichaichai' on a loop on the trains, where it is served in small home-made clay cups. The tracks are littered with shattered clay from disposed cups. Indian *chai* is always sweet and milky.

Whenever I go to a festival, especially Glastonbury, I head for the *chai* teepee. *Chai* is a warming, feel-good drink, great in a flask at an outdoor event or picnic if the weather isn't looking too good.

To make *chai*, first of all you need to make an Indian spice mixture called *chai masala*. Everybody has their own *chai* spice mix for the tea, this is mine.

First, put together your *chai masala* mix. Add the boiling water to a pot, along with the tea and *chai masala* mix. Simmer for 5–10 minutes, then scoop out the tea unless you like it very strong. Add the condensed milk, and palm sugar or jaggery, to taste.

Flower Tea

These are very pretty. They are expensive, at about £1.50 each, but worth the cost. I recommend investing in a glass teapot just to see the extraordinary blossom unfurl (see stockists on page 250).

Simply drop a flower 'bomb' into a glass teapot and pour just-boiled water (around 85°C) on top. Watch as the flower expands and grows within the pot. Pour into a fine china cup to drink.

Lemongrass Tea

Easy peasy. I tried this in one of the ramen bars that have become very fashionable in London. Amazing.

You just submerge a stick of lemongrass in a cup of hot water. Job done. Refreshing, thirst-quenching, healthy. I keep my lemongrass in the freezer and retrieve individual sticks whenever I need one for recipes or a pot of tea.

Hibiscus Tea *(Flor de Jamaica)*

Buy a large bag of dried hibiscus blooms and keep them next to your kettle. Pop 4 or 5 flower heads in a cup of boiling water. Hibiscus is full of vitamin C, it is the secret ingredient in Celestial Seasonings Red Zinger Tea, and drinking 3 cups a day has been proved to lower blood pressure. Sweeten with agave syrup or stevia if you want to keep it healthy.

Mint Tea

Makes 2–3 cups

2 tsp gunpowder tea leaves
500ml just-boiled water (around 85°C)
Sugar, to taste
A large bunch of fresh mint
    or spearmint leaves
Pine nuts, for sprinkling

I drank mint tea often when I lived in Paris in the 20th arron-dissement. It was there that Edith Piaf sang while straddling the cobblestones of Belleville at the beginning of her career. Cafés have generous space outside for tables and chairs on the wide boulevard of Menilmouche. Fresh mint tea is served in cheap or-nate glasses called *keesan*, and silvery metal teapots called *bred*, then sprinkled with pine nuts. In Moroccan tea culture, mint tea is made with green or gunpowder (which is like tiny pellets) tea. I also like to make it with just a handful of fresh mint leaves and sugar to taste. It aids digestion, too.

Add the gunpowder tea (a type of green tea) to the just-boiled wa-ter. Steep the tea for 5 minutes, then strain out the leaves and add sugar to taste. Moroccans love sweet tea, so don't hold back. Bring to the boil for a few minutes, then add the fresh mint leaves. The pot should be stuffed with fresh mint.

Like pulled tea, you serve this from on high into glasses so that the tea is aerated and gets a foam on top. Sprinkle with a few pine nuts on top, and serve.

Orange Blossom Tea

This is not so much a tea as what the French call a *tisane* – merely recently boiled water poured over the delicate orange blossom flowers and, if desired, a little sugar. I had it in Seville at the house of a supper club hostess. (Seville is the most beautiful city in the world, filled with the fragrant blossom of orange trees, white horses and tiny backstreet tapas bars.) A few orange blossoms in hot water are very cleansing after a meal.

Steep 1 or 2 fresh orange blossoms per cup in hot (not quite boiling) water and leave to steep for a few minutes. You can leave the blos-soms in when drinking.

Cherry Blossom Tea

There are some nationalities in the world that like, bizarrely to our tastes, salty tea. One such people is the Tibetans who drink black tea with salt and yak butter. I spent some months in Tibet and eventually, after being offered it everywhere, especially at Buddhist monasteries, I learnt to enjoy their salty, buttery tea. Another salty tea is from Japan and it uses pickled cherry blossoms, called *sakura*, which you can buy online (see stockists on page 250). It is both fragrant and savoury. You could also use fresh cherry blossoms when they are in season.

Shake the salt off 3 or 4 pickled cherry blossoms per cup. Add hot water (not quite boiling) to the blossoms and leave to steep for 3–5 minutes. Leave the blossoms in while drinking, it's a very pretty cup of tea with the floating pink petals.

You can also use the leaves from sour cherry trees, as well as leaves from olive trees. Just infuse the leaves in just-boiled water for 3–5 minutes.

Chocolate Tea

Makes 2–3 cups

2 balls of Caribbean chocolate
  (see stockists on page 250) or 75g good-
  quality unsweetened cocoa powder
500ml boiling water
1 cinnamon stick
Sugar, to taste
A pinch of ground nutmeg, or to taste
Milk or cream, to taste
White overproof rum (optional)

I have an enterprising Jamaican neighbour, MsRiceandPeas, who has started a small food business selling Caribbean food on Fridays outside the school gates to other mums. She introduced me to chocolate tea, which is thinner than hot chocolate. It's made with boiling water rather than milk and uses authentic, but rough, chocolate, very similar to the 'cakes' of chocolate sold in countries like Bolivia. You can find this sold in kits in Caribbean shops, with pastilles of real chocolate and large cinnamon leaves. Here is how to make it yourself.

Combine the chocolate, boiling water and cinnamon stick in a pan and simmer for 3–5 minutes. Add sugar and nutmeg to taste. Strain the tea before serving, adding the milk or cream last. Some Jamaican ladies like to add a dash of white overproof rum.

Tea Accessories

A formal afternoon tea requires a tea strainer, a milk jug and a sugar bowl. If you are using sugar cubes, then sugar tongs are needed.

Sugar Sugar

Don't forget the sugar! This too can be beautiful with home-made crafty touches. You can make your own wrappers, your own flavoured sugar cubes (see below), or decorate ready-made ones. Another tip: find crystallised sugar on a stick in Middle Eastern shops in either plain white or gold with saffron strands. You can also make your own floral or botanical sugars: infuse a bag of sugar with lavender, rose, lilac or lemon geranium petals, or flavour it with cinnamon sticks, citrus peel or vanilla pods. Simply mix your chosen flower or spice into a jar of sugar and leave it to absorb the scent. Not only do these ideas look good, but they also add flavour to drinks and baked goods.

Flavoured Sugar Cubes

Makes 12 x 1cm² cubes

150g white granulated sugar per flavour
1 tsp flavouring such as rose water, orange-blossom water, or fresh lemon juice
1 tsp water
Food colouring of your choice (I use pink for the rose water and orange for the orange-blossom water)

You'd be surprised how very simple it is to make your own sugar cubes, plus it gives your tea party a hand-made rustic look, while the different flavours add something extra to the taste of your tea.

Put the sugar into a large bowl. In a separate small cup, combine the flavouring, water and food colouring. Pour this mixture into the sugar and mix thoroughly until evenly combined.

Pour the flavoured sugar on to a parchment paper-lined baking sheet or a silicone mat and pat it into a compact rectangle. Use a bench scraper or knife to cut the block across in rows and then again in columns to create approximately 1cm² cubes. Leave to dry for about 30 minutes then separate gently and let dry for an additional 20 minutes. When completely dry, store in an airtight container.

Make Your Own Tea Bags

You can make your own tea bags, ensuring that you have just the tea you want, or you can decorate tea bags you already have. Here are a few ideas:

- Buy empty tea bags and fill your own. These biodegradable empty tea bags are readily available online (see stockists on page 250). You can buy cup-sized or pot-sized bags. Some just flap over and others come with a string to tighten.
- It's easy to tailor your own tea or herbal blend. Mix dried rose petals, dried citrus peels, unsweetened cocoa powder, olive leaves (either fresh or dried), dried camomile petals and different types of tea.
- Decorate the tags or add your own. You can replace the tag on a tea bag by adding some decorative washi tape (a Japanese masking tape, available online, that comes in beautiful patterns and colours and which you can write on) or completely replace the tag. Make them from cardboard and name your blend, or write slogans such as 'dump that guy', 'propertea is theft', 'down with tea tax', other suitable snippets of advice, or simply 'enjoy tea'.

Decorated Sugar Cubes

Makes about 100 decorated sugar cubes

About 100 plain white sugar cubes

FOR THE ROYAL ICING
*(you will need less than the quantity this
makes, so perhaps make these at the same
time you have something to ice)*
1 egg white
250g icing sugar, sifted
Food colouring in different colours

EQUIPMENT
Several small, sealable airtight bowls
*Several disposable piping bags, one for
    each colour (small ones are easier to
    manage)*
*Parchment paper-lined baking sheet or a
    silicone mat*
*Toothpicks or cocktail sticks to help
    nudge around the tiny amounts of icing*

This is the same principle as cupcake decorating, but you have to imagine tiny doll's-house cupcakes. You can use sprinkles, pearls or sugar stars, or any of the cake decorations you find in shops, then mix up tiny amounts of royal icing to stick them on with.

First, make the royal icing. Whisk the egg white in a bowl until stiff, then add the icing sugar, folding it in until combined and smooth. Immediately divide the icing into the bowls, mixing a drop or two of food colouring into each one, leaving one white. Cover and seal.

Fill each piping bag with one of the coloured icings, snip off the tip and then with the first colour, pipe the shape of flower petals on to the parchment paper. Fill the centre with a second colour. Repeat to make lots of colourful icing flowers.

Leave your icing flowers to dry, then, using the white icing, stick the decorations on to the sugar cubes, using toothpicks to help nudge around the icing, if necessary. Leave to dry again. Store in an air-tight container.

Place a couple of decorated sugar cubes on each saucer and serve with a nice cup of tea.

Make Your Own Sugar Cube Wraps

Creating your own sugar cube wraps is the perfect way to add some of your personality and humour to the tea table. Use the template below to create your own designs; mine features a gaggle of tea-drinking ladies, but yours could feature any design that takes your fancy. Text works very well and it can be fun to write messages that run around the cubes.

To make your own, copy out the template and create your design on the back.

Place the wrap, design-side down, on a flat surface and put two sugar cubes in the centre. Parcel them up like a present, so that the design wraps around the sides.

If you are struggling to figure out the best way to fold them, there are plenty of tutorials online, or at **msmarmitelover.com.**

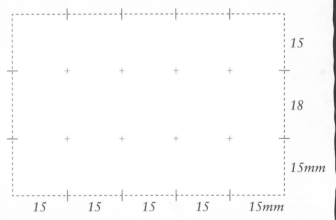

15

18

15mm

15   15   15   15   15mm

My tea drinking ladies. Find more templates at **msmarmitelover.com.**
Tip: For my template, I used Tate & Lyle sugar cubes, which measure 15 x 15 x 18mm.

- - - - - - - - - - - - - - - - - - - = Cut
————————————— = Fold

Tea Without Tea

Some drinks will make their way into your tea party regardless of convention. Here are a few of my favourites:

Hot Chocolate

Makes 2 cups

2 tsp good-quality unsweetened cocoa powder
500ml milk
50g Green & Black's Mayan Gold chocolate, or any good-quality orange-flavoured or dark chocolate, broken into chunks
30g good-quality milk chocolate, broken into chunks
1 cinnamon stick
1 vanilla pod, or a couple of drops of vanilla extract
¼ tsp ground nutmeg
A pinch of sea salt
50g caster or soft light brown sugar
50ml double cream
2 tsp grated chocolate or unsweetened cocoa powder, to dust

OPTIONS
Ginger Hot Chocolate: same as above but add ½ teaspoon ground ginger to the mixture while heating it up, and then add 1 teaspoon or more of chopped candied ginger to each cup on top of the whipped cream, when serving.
White Hot Chocolate: same as above but replace the milk chocolate with good-quality white chocolate and leave some for grating on top.

The best hot chocolate I ever drank was in Mougins, in the south of France. We baulked at the price – 6 euros (almost £6) – but when it arrived we could see it was worth every centime. For a start, it was in a bowl the size of a large soup dish, it came with another large bowl filled with whipped cream, and it used no less than three different types of chocolate in its construction. I asked for the recipe but the owner wouldn't give it to me. This is the nearest I can get to it.

Put the cocoa powder in a pan with a little of the milk and stir to make a paste. Set the pan over a medium heat and slowly add the rest of the milk while whisking to add frothiness.

Add all the chocolate pieces, continuing to stir until melted, followed by the cinnamon stick, vanilla pod, nutmeg and salt. Continue to heat but do not let the mixture boil, then remove from the heat and add the sugar, adding a little more if you like it sweeter. To my taste, 50g was the perfect amount.

In the meantime, whip the cream in a bowl to form soft peaks.

Remove and discard the cinnamon stick and vanilla pod. Pour the hot chocolate into mugs or, for that French chic style, small deep bowls, spoon a large scoop of whipped cream on top of each one, then sprinkle with the grated chocolate or cocoa powder.

You could use whipped cream from a can, but I find once I have a can of that stuff in my house, I start shooting it straight into my mouth like drugs.

Russian Hot Jam 'Tea'

This will sound weird but it's actually very good. I had it at Mari Vanna, an extraordinary Russian restaurant in London where the interior looks like a Russian grannie's living room, full of dolls and vintage china and enormous glass jars of home-made pickles. Yes, it's fussy and over the top, but I love it. It's worth going there just to people-watch; Russian ballerinas, crazy violinists, old rich men with thin young women taking 'selfies' at the table. The women all wear furs and teetering red-soled shoes, they have incredible bone structure, and rather a few of them enter carrying giant bouquets as if they've just come off stage. I was munching my way through the menu and spotted hot jam tea. 'What's that like?' I asked the stern Slavic waitress. Her face softened. 'It is good, I bring you a cup you can try.'

She brought a silvery teapot filled with hot water and three bowls of jam – blackcurrant, raspberry and apricot. The black-currant was like hot Ribena, and the others the equivalent but in different flavours. Mind blown.

Simply add 2–3 tablespoons of jam of your choice to 1 cup of boiling water and stir.

Teatime Cocktails

Along with refreshing and healthy cups of tea, you do need something to perk up the conversation at a tea party and loosen things up a bit. Here are some teatime cocktails for you to consider:

Regent Punch

Serves 16

50ml water
350g caster sugar
1 pineapple, peeled and cored,
    then half the flesh cubed and the rest
    sliced for the bowl
250ml dark rum, plus 2 tbsp
4 tbsp or 4 bags of green tea
Pared rinds and juice of 4 lemons
    (make sure there is no white pith left on
    the rinds)
800ml just-boiled water,
    left to sit for 1 minute
Pared rinds and juice of 2 oranges, Seville
    if in season, plus extra slices for the bowl
350ml brandy or cognac
Ice cubes
2 bottles (75cl each) brut champagne

GLASS TYPE
Punch cup

The name punch derives from the hindi word for 'five', *panch*, because it usually contains at least five constituent ingredients.

It's almost worth investing in a punch set for this elegant cocktail that was imbibed regularly, and in great quantity, by the Prince Regent George Augustus Frederick (later George IV), after whom it was named. It includes tea.

You will need to start making this punch the night before your tea party.

Put the water and 50g of the sugar in a small pan over a low heat, stirring until the sugar dissolves, to make a sugar syrup. Remove from the heat and leave to cool, then pour into a bowl, add the pineapple cubes and the 2 tablespoons of rum and leave to infuse overnight.

The next day, steep the tea with the pared lemon rinds in the just-boiled water for 5 minutes. Strain into a large bowl. Add the infused pineapple cube mixture, the remaining 300g sugar, the lemon juice, orange rinds and juice, brandy and the remaining rum, stirring to combine. This will keep in the fridge for a couple of weeks.

When ready to serve, add the ice cubes, champagne and the pineapple and orange slices.

Teapot Cocktails

Be a secret drinker. Teapot cocktails are a sneaky way of adding more alcohol to your event and always a great way to kick things off. Innocent bystanders will just think you are drinking plenty of tea.

My suggestion is to pour these cocktails into clean teapots and top them up as and when. While my largest teapot contains 800ml and my smallest 150ml, the average teapot contains 500ml. The average teacup contains 150ml, so I will suggest servings in terms of cups and you can adjust this to the size of your teapot.

If you have a small tea party or guests who don't drink, all of these cocktails will last virtually indefinitely, except for the soft-drink element, which will go flat, so they can be used on another occasion. Only pour in the soft drink when you are about to serve.

Teapot Bucks Fizz

Makes enough for a couple of teapots
(I can guarantee you'll want top ups)

2 tangerines, clementines, mandarins or
  satsumas, peeled, segmented and each
  segment stripped of pith
1 bottle (75cl) champagne, cava or prosecco
300ml freshly squeezed orange juice

EQUIPMENT
2 or more ice-cube trays

Make your mind up to buy a glass teapot at last (see stockists on page 250), that way you can see the bubbles!

Place a small tangerine, clementine, mandarin or satsuma segment into each compartment of an ice-cube tray and top up with champagne, cava or prosecco. Freeze until firm.

Pour the orange juice and the remaining champagne into a glass teapot, or at least a very-clean-on-the-inside ceramic/china one. Add the ice cubes and serve.

If you don't have a glass teapot, put the ice cubes straight into the teacups instead.

Peach Iced 'Tea'

Makes 4 cups

2 tea bags, such as orange pekoe or other
  black tea
300ml just-boiled water
4 tbsp caster sugar
50ml peach schnapps
50ml vodka
50ml peach nectar juice
1 fresh peach, halved and stoned

This is a classic Southern drink with an extra bit of fun thrown in. Scarlett O'Hara would have sipped on this while plotting how to trap her next beau. This one could also be made in a jug.

Steep the tea bags in the just-boiled water. Once the tea is at the strength you require, remove the tea bags, then stir in the sugar, wait until it cools, then add the alcohol and peach nectar juice.

Cut the peach halves into small segments, putting all but four of the segments into the teapot or jug, then make a little slit down the centre of the two remaining segments. Pour the peach tea into the cups and arrange a slit peach segment on the edge of each cup.

Tea Totaller

Makes 10 cups

½ bottle (35cl) vodka
4 tbsp white mulberry tea or other good
   tea leaves
Chilled tonic water, to serve
Strips of pared lemon rind, to serve
Caster sugar, to taste

You can do more things with tea leaves than just boil them. Here is a tea-infused cocktail, which looks beautiful served from a glass teapot. Astringent and refreshing on a summer's day; add a strip of pared lemon rind and a spoonful of sugar to each cup.

Infuse the vodka by adding the tea leaves to the bottle of vodka and leaving it to marinate for 2 days. Strain, discarding the tea, and then return the vodka to the bottle. Leave the tea-flavoured vodka in the freezer for a couple of hours before serving.

To serve, pour a few measures of the tea-flavoured vodka, say 35ml (just over 2 tablespoons) per person, into a teapot and top up the pot with the tonic water. The ratio is normally 1:3 so for 35ml of vodka, you'll add 100ml of chilled tonic water. Measure the volume of your teapot and add the amount of vodka and tonic water necessary. Pour into teacups, then add a strip of pared lemon rind and a spoonful of sugar to each cup.

Mother's Ruin

Makes 2 cups

120ml gin, chilled in the freezer
50ml elderflower syrup or St Germain
   elderflower liqueur
150ml chilled tonic water

Since the popularity of gin rose in the 17th century, when reduced taxes meant that women could drink alongside men, gin has always been a woman's drink. Hogarth captured this in his engravings featuring women neglecting their maternal duties, hence the nickname for gin 'Mother's Ruin'. There has always been a double standard about women enjoying a drink. You could say that moral panic, gin and feminism go together: American evangelist Pat Robertson once said that feminism is a movement that encourages women to leave their husbands, kill their children, practise witchcraft, destroy capitalism and become lesbians. I can't guarantee any of that but a measure of equality sure slips down nicely.

Pour the ice-cold gin into the teapot, add the elderflower syrup and tonic water and stir.

Cordials and Hedgerow Liqueurs

I've always wanted an old-fashioned pantry. There is something very alluring about rows of glass containers, glinting with jewel-like colours, bulging with something rich and intoxicating. Instead, I have a cupboard under the stairs where, in the darkness, lurk dozens of bottles and jars, each prettily labelled. Some I will give as gifts, while some have been there for years, to be dusted off for Christmas or an occasion such as an afternoon tea. This little 'pantry' makes me feel as if I'm ready for anything, even nuclear war. Many of the jars contain fruit in liqueur or bottled cordials. These concoctions last for a year or more. The ideal pantry should be dark, dry and fairly cool. Here are a few recipes to get your pantry started:

Crème de Cassis/Crème de Mûre

Makes 2.5 litres

450g ripe blackcurrants or blackberries
1 bottle (75cl) good red wine
1kg caster sugar
1 bottle (70cl) vodka

EQUIPMENT
Jelly bag or piece of muslin cloth
2.5 litres of sterilised bottles (see page 41)
  May I suggest making a big 1 litre bottle for yourself and packing the rest in 500ml bottles for presents? (A litre bottle will see you through many kir royals or otherwise.)

A measure of blackcurrant cassis or blackberry mûre liqueur in a glass of champagne or white wine is a French classic (kir royal). For kir royal, use 15ml (1 tablespoon) crème de cassis for each glass of champagne or white wine. It's a simple cocktail often used as an aperitif, but also a lovely way of sweetening some fizz at an afternoon tea.

You could also tip small amounts of crème de cassis into tiny sherry glasses and sip at it. Make a nice label or tag for a flip-top bottle, decorate with a ribbon and you have a gift for a friend. You could also use this as a topping for ice cream.

Wash the fruit, place it in a large glass jar or bowl and crush with a wooden spoon. Or, you can pulse it slightly in a food processor, just to burst the skins. Add the red wine, cover it and leave to macerate for 48 hours.

Strain the fruity wine, discarding the flesh. Add the sugar. Pour into a stainless steel pan and simmer over a medium heat for at least 30 minutes, until it becomes syrupy, stirring with a wooden spoon from time to time.

Remove from the heat and leave to cool to blood temperature, then filter the syrup into a jug through a jelly bag or muslin cloth placed over a sieve. Don't press down but let the weight of the syrup seep through at its own pace.

Add the vodka to the strained syrup and stir to mix, then funnel the 'crème' into the sterilised bottles and seal.

Sloe or Damson Gin

Makes 1 litre

500g sloes or damsons, pricked all over
  (so they absorb the alcohol)
250g caster sugar
1 bottle (70cl) gin

EQUIPMENT

1.5-litre sterilised Kilner jar (see page 41)
1 litre sterilised bottle (see page 41),
  or you could use 2 x 500ml bottles
  or other pretty bottles (sterilised, of
  course) and give this as a gift

Sloe gin is terribly expensive so have a go at making your own; it's easy to make and you'll be so proud. It's great for gifts as well as tea party tipples. Addictive stuff.

Tip all the ingredients into the Kilner jar and stir to mix, then seal and keep in a dark cupboard. Leave for 6 months to a year. Every so often shake the jar.

After 6 months, strain the alcohol from the fruit (the fruit can be used in trifles or combined with whipped cream and meringue). Using a funnel, pour the alcohol into a pretty sterilised bottle or two and seal. Add a label and ribbon if you're planning to give them as gifts.

Hot Toddies

I'm writing this book during a summer heatwave when all I can think about is cool drinks. It's easy to forget that most of the year in the UK, during autumn, winter and spring, what we want is a hot toddy. Winters for the last few years have been long. Drinks like these cheer the soul.

Hot Gin

Makes 1.5 litres

This is a simple version of Charles Dickens' Gin Punch.

1 lemon, thinly sliced
A handful of whole cloves
1 bottle (70cl) gin
750ml hot water
6 allspice berries
300g caster sugar

Stud the lemon slices with the cloves, then mix all the ingredients together in a large pan and simmer for 15 minutes. Remove from the heat, then serve. No need to strain unless your guests don't like 'bits'.

Harvest Cider

Makes about 4.5 litres
(enough for a large party, about 20 people)

2 litres unsweetened apple juice
2 litres sweet cider
250g soft dark brown sugar
8 cinnamon sticks
    (plus extra for serving one in each
    glass – optional)
3 eating apples, cored and sliced
    ½ bottle (35cl) bourbon, Jack Daniels,
    Southern Comfort or grain alcohol

I made this for my *Little House on the Prairie* dinner. As it was snowing outside, this glowing drink created a lovely, hospitable atmosphere as guests arrived. There is a similar British version traditionally drunk at this time of year called Wassail, which uses ale rather than cider.

This is ideal for serving at a tea party or party, but halve the recipe if you have fewer guests, although I usually find anything mulled seems to slip down fast.

Put the apple juice, cider, sugar, cinnamon sticks and apple slices in a pan and bring to the boil, then immediately reduce to a simmer and simmer for 5 minutes.

Remove from the heat and leave it to cool, then stir in the bourbon or other alcohol. Warm again and serve. You can reuse the cinnamon sticks and put one in each glass, if you like.

Lavender Gin Toddy

Serves 8

100ml honey
4 or 5 fresh or dried lavender sprigs
350ml gin (or one 35cl half bottle)
Juice of 4 lemons
350ml hot water

Fresh or dried lavender sprigs,
  one to decorate each glass

I first made this for the monthly Sunday afternoon supper club I run, called The Secret Garden Club, set in my garden. Myself and my colleague, Zia Mays, do a gardening workshop or demonstration of how to make something, then I cook a high tea from the ingredients. I concocted this drink when we were showing original recipes for herbs from your garden. Lavender and gin are a potent floral combination.

Put the honey and lavender sprigs into a small pan over a low heat. Heat gently until hot (but do not let the mixture boil), then remove from the heat and leave to infuse for a couple of hours. Warm the mixture again when you are ready to finish and serve the drink.

Warm up the gin, lemon juice and hot water (add more hot water for a weaker cocktail) in a pan, with the honey and lavender infusion. If it isn't sweet enough, feel free to add more honey. Serve warm in glasses, decorating each glass with a lavender sprig. No need to strain before serving.

Tip: Make lavender sugar with any unused leftover lavender sprigs by adding the sprigs to a bag or jar of sugar and leaving it for a few weeks to infuse.

Useful Books

101 Sandwiches: A Collection of the Finest
Sandwich Recipes from Around the World
Helen Graves (Dog and Bone)
Fantastic South London/Peckham-based food blogger who has written a brilliant tome about sandwiches from around the world. Some of them are appalling and others are delicious. Inspirational.

A New System of Domestic Cookery
Mrs Rundell (Persephone)
Good British recipes and household tips from an early 19th-century Delia. Good on cookery for the poor and directions for servants.

Adventures with Chocolate: 80 Sensational Recipes
Paul A. Young (Kyle Books)
London chocolatier, an authority on chocolate. Gorgeous book.

Cressida Bell's Cake Design: Fifty Fabulous Cakes
Cressida Bell and Sonja Reed (Double-Barrelled Books)
Artist decorates cakes, and how! Intricate, beautiful designs.

The Duchess of Devonshire's Chatsworth Cookery Book
The Duchess of Devonshire (Frances Lincoln)
The last of the Mitford girls – not the fascist one or the communist one, but the aristocratic one. A descendant by marriage of the woman that started this whole afternoon tea malarkey. A taster from the book: 'I haven't cooked since the war.'

First Preserves: Marmalades, Jams, Chutneys
Vivien Lloyd (Citrus Press)
Clear, concise jam making book.

The Free Range Cook
Annabel Langbein (Mitchell Beazley)
A New Zealand-based cook. Lovely recipes in this book. I riffed on her cloud cake recipe for my Passion Fruit Cloud Cake.

How to be a Domestic Goddess :
Baking and the Art of Comfort Cooking
Nigella Lawson (Chatto & Windus)
Worship her, for this millennial book, published in 2000, kick-started a generation of women to realise it was OK to be home-makers again.

Je Veux du Chocolat!
Trish Deseine (Marabout)
The queen of chocolate is an Irishwoman styling it up in Paris. Beautiful books; this one made her famous all over France, quite a feat.

Jelly by Bompas & Parr
Sam Bompas and Harry Parr (Pavilion)
Foodie pioneers who resuscitated jelly and made it revolutionary.

The Little Book of Scones
Liam D'Arcy and Grace Hall (Square Peg)
Sconetastic duo who sell in London food markets. They're pushing the envelope with their avant-garde scone flavours.

Love in a Cold Climate
Nancy Mitford
Witty writing; read this to get yourself in the mood for an afternoon tea party.

Henrietta Lovell, the Rare Tea Lady
So far she hasn't written a book but I hope she will. The British authority on good tea.

Meringue Girls Cookbook
Alex Hoffler and Stacey O'Gorman (Square Peg)
Fun bright book for those who are meringue aficionados.

Pastry: Savoury and Sweet
Michel Roux (Quadrille)
All the books in this series (Eggs, Desserts, Sauces) are good. I got my basic choux recipe from his book. Handy little reference books with rock-solid recipes.

The Perfect Scoop: Ice Creams, Sorbets,
Granitas and Sweet Accompaniments
David Lebovitz (Jacqui Small)
Brilliant Paris-based blogger and former pastry chef has written an ice cream bible.

Supper Club: Recipes and Notes
from the Underground Restaurant
Kerstin Rodgers (Collins)
Well if I don't big up my own books, who will? If you are interested in starting an afternoon tea supper club, this book will tell you how.

Secret Tea Rooms

SECRET TEA ROOMS IN ENGLAND

BATH

The Secret Tea Party

Mrs Stokes does pop up vintage teas around Bath (also in Bristol, Cheltenham, Oxford or the Cotswolds). She does a very moist carrot cake and makes mini versions of large cakes, for instance mini Victoria sponges.
www.secretteaparty.com

BRISTOL AND SURROUNDING AREA

Bishopston Supper Club
Bristol

Danielle Coombs is the chef and hostess of the Bishopston Supper Club: she also does quarterly secret tea parties in her living room. Children are welcome. Her signature cake is probably a 'boozy chocolate, cherry and cream sponge' or perhaps 'a spiced orange and almond cake'.
www.restingchef.wordpress.com

Peachie Vintage
Rickford, Yeo Valley

Anna Brooman, the real name of Peachie Vintage, does secret teas at her home in Rickford, Yeo Valley, and elsewhere, every 6 weeks. She changes her menu at each tea party, but her salted caramel and apple macarons are always popular.
www.peachievintage.com

CHESHIRE

Pretty Little Trio's Secret Vintage Tea Party (pop up)
Stockton Heath, Cheshire

Rebecca Jenkinson runs bi-monthly secret teas, which is incredible considering she is also bringing up young triplets. So the 'pretty little trio' has two meanings: her triplets, and also a teacup/saucer/teaplate set is known to vintage china collectors as a 'trio'. Rebecca has a passion for vintage china.
www.prettylittletrio.co.uk

Violet's Vintage Teas
Grappenhall, Cheshire

Named after a great grandmother, these ladies host regular midweek afternoon tea parties at their homes. They loan vintage hats, gloves and bags for guests to wear.
www.facebook.com/violetsvintageteas

DERBYSHIRE

Rachael's Secret Tea Room
Belper, Derbyshire

Rachael's secret teas are held in a quiet setting on the edge of the Peak District in Derbyshire. Her tea room is open on the last Saturday of every month, but she can also take bookings on Friday and Saturday afternoons. She can host up to 8 guests. On a cake level, Rachael loves anything lemony.
www.rachaelssecrettearoom.co.uk

Vintage Rose Tea Party
Chesterfield, Derbyshire

Victoria Almarresh hosts regular pop up secret vintage tea parties, but is looking for premises to expand her small business. Her signature cake is a rose water cake.
www.vintagerosecatering.com

LONDON

Alice's Tea Garden
Chorleywood, South West London

Kristie hosts secret tea parties at her home in Chorleywood but will also go to your own home to create your afternoon tea or tea tasting.
www.alicesteagarden.com

Jaim's Kitchen
South London

Malaysian food blogger and patisserie chef Jaim hosts secret teas at her house in South London. She makes a 'mean genoise sponge with different fillings' and a highly praised 'chocolate, pear and salted caramel cake'.
www.jaimskitchen.blogspot.co.uk

La Sagra Secret Tea
Putney/Wandsworth

Angie is a former sound engineer who has spent many years in Italy. She's also a keen baker and, tired of the anonymity and high prices of London hotel afternoon teas, has opened up her home for secret teas. Freshly baked scones are always on the menu.
www.la-sagra.com

Maison Mari
Nunhead, London

Hostess Helena Appio creates pop up afternoon teas both in her 1930s house and in quirky venues around South London. Her teas are themed upon the 1930s' to the 1960s' eras and she specialises in cake decoration, especially delicate sugar flowers.
www.maisonmari.com

The Hidden Tea Room
Putney, South West London

Milli and Vic share a passion for cooking and baking and have started a monthly tea room in their sitting room. They have an open kitchen so are looking forward to nattering with their guests as they prepare the tea. Their favourite cake is 'chocolate and boozy'.
www.milliskitchen.blogspot.co.uk

The Underground Restaurant
Kilburn, London

Run by MsMarmitelover; occasional secret teas as well as her ground-breaking supper club. Her signature bake is pavlovas.
www.msmarmitelover.com

Yummy Choos
Croydon, South London

Selina Periampillai does afternoon teas at her supper club 'Yummy Choos' in Croydon. She will sometimes bake classic Mauritian cakes such as purine mais (polenta cake), gateaux palate (sweet potato dough filled with coconut) and napolitaines (shortbread biscuits, filled with jam and covered in pink icing).
www.yummychooeats.com

Bloomsbury Teas
Kingston-on-Thames
Bloomsbury Teas is a tea party hosted and baked by David Herbert who is an Australian cookbook author and former editor of a vast range of food magazines in the UK. He's a well known collector of Bloomsbury-era ceramics and furniture. If you go to his tea party, you will be sitting on chairs, the covers of which have been hand sewn by Virginia Woolf, and original 1920s' crockery. At present he seats six people and you must book out the entire tea party. Today David styles food and does the prop styling for some top food writers while continuing with his own cookbooks. You will be in for a treat with this afternoon tea, fantastic baking, beautiful surroundings and excellent gossip.
www.bloomsburyteas.com

MANCHESTER

The Gourmand's Secret Vintage Afternoon Tea Party
Manchester
Laura hosts secret teas once every 6 weeks at secret locations in Manchester.
www.facebook.com/vintagegourmand

Vintage Afternoon Teas
Bowdon, Manchester suburbs
Gwyneth Brock welcomes you to her monthly secret tea room at her home, an 18th-century former farmhouse. (She also 'pops up' around Cheshire.) She sometimes collaborates with others such as veggie/ vegan chefs or with local crafter Jo to run secret crafternoon tea parties.
www.vintageafternoonteas.co.uk

NOTTINGHAMSHIRE

Lotties Secret Tea Room
Nottinghamshire
Nottingham Lottie welcomes guests to her secret tea room at her home. Her speciality is themed cupcakes.
about.me/lotties
or *www.facebook.com/Lotties*

OXFORDSHIRE

The Secret Teapot
Thame, Oxfordshire
Vicky Sponge, the pseudonym of retired professional chef Ann Parsons, saw a secret tea room as an enjoyable way to carry on with her first love: baking. 'Baking is for sharing', she says. Her conservatory dining/tea room is open most Saturday afternoons, so do check out her website to pre-book. She can fit in 10 guests. Everything is served on vintage china.
www.thesecretteapot.co.uk

SURREY

Tea Time Treats
Ewell, Surrey
Jane Cakelady runs monthly afternoon teas from her dining room. She uses vintage china. Her customers really love her scones and her award-winning 'Best in Show' Victoria sponge. She can fit up to 12 people. She can also bring her afternoon tea to your place.
www.teatimecakelady.co.uk

WEST YORKSHIRE

Café Nouveau
Huddersfield
The lightest baking from Marie-Claire Micuta at her home. Secret teas are held monthly with up to 8 guests. Her signature cake is her peach and blueberry cake.
cafenouveau.wordpress.com

Chez Shamwari
Saltaire
Shirley Quarmby runs a regular secret tea room. She also does gluten-free baking.
www.chezshamwari.com

WILTSHIRE

The Utterly Sexy Cafe
Tisbury
Amanda Baird does beautifully decorated cakes along with her exquisite vintage tea sets and cake plates at her home in Tisbury, Wiltshire. Her signature cake is earl grey tea and cardamom cake with whisky icing.
www.utterlysexycafe.co.uk

SECRET TEA ROOMS IN SCOTLAND

DUMFRIES AND GALLOWAY

Dix Blue
Lockerbie
Carolyn Richardson is a famed poet and secret tea hostess. She also does tea events combined with writers and poets speaking.
seraphimin.wix.com/dixblue

EAST LOTHIAN AND EDINBURGH

High Societea
East Lothian
Jan Ogilvie hosts monthly pop up teas around her area, sometimes in her garden, often in country houses and garden centres. She even does funeral teas! Some of her grieving customers, widowers, ask for cakes that their wives baked when they were alive. 'One gentleman asked me for a cherry cake, as that was what his wife made', Jan told me.
www.highsocieteas.co.uk

The Queen of Tarts
Edinburgh
Angela Dolan runs a pop up tea room at various locations in Edinburgh. Her light-as-air shortbread towers are celebrated.
www.facebook.com/QueenofTartsEdinburgh

 SECRET TEA ROOMS ABROAD

ARGENTINA

Eclaire–El arte de té at Casa Munet
Buenos Aires
Tea expert Pedro and pastry chef Virginia Rinaldi host a weekly private afternoon tea.
www.eclaire.com.ar

SWEDEN

Hemma Hos Linn
Stockholm
Linn Soderstrom mostly runs an evening supper club. You can book via her website.
www.hemmahoslinn.se

Please look for updated details on Secret Tea Rooms by going to 'Find a Supper Club' website:
www.supperclubfangroup.ning.com

Useful Contacts and Stockists: Ingredients

Amedei chocolate: *www.kingsfinefood.co.uk*

Authentic ingredients for the Jamaican Chocolate Tea recipe: *www.bluemountainpeak.com*

Chestnut flour: *www.goodnessdirect.co.uk* (Shipton Mill flours)

Citric acid: this can be found in Asian shops or from *www.amazon.co.uk*

Couverture: *www.souschef.co.uk*

Culinary dried lavender: *www.steenbergs.co.uk*

Culinary (food grade) lavender oil: *www.healthysupplies.co.uk*

Dried hibiscus flowers: *www.melburyandappleton.co.uk*

Easy-melt chocolate: *www.squires-shop.com*

Fondant icing: *www.almondart.com*

High quality tea: *www.rareteacompany.com*

Lemon marmalade with lavender: *www.ousevalleyfoods.com*

Light corn syrup: *www.amazon.co.uk*

Nibbed pistachios: Persepolis, Peckham, London *www.foratasteofpersia.co.uk*

Pandan essence (also known as bai toey or screwpine): *www.theasiancookshop.co.uk*

Pickled cherry blossoms: *www.anything-from-japan.com* or *www.amazon.co.uk*

Sachets of Fizz Whiz: *www.amazon.co.uk*

Sticks of hard liquorice candy: Fox's Spices *Tel 01789 266420* (also on Facebook)

Transfer sheets: *www.thecakedecoratingcompany.co.uk*

Vanilla sugar: *www.steenbergs.co.uk*

Useful Contacts and Stockists: Equipment

Acetate sheets (for Chocolate Teacups recipe): *www.lisabdesigns.co.uk*

Brigitte Keks biscuit-printing sets: *www.amazon.co.uk*

Chocolate tea cake moulds (silicone cake mould with 6 half sphere indentations – for Lavender Temari Cakes recipe), baking tins, jam jars, mini madeleine mould, pretty preserving bottles, mould for assembling Pastel Croquembouche recipe: *www.lakeland.co.uk*

Craft supplies and much more (including oasis ball for Sweet Tree recipe): *www.hobbycraft.co.uk* or *www.cngfloristsundries.co.uk* (many florists and garden centres also stock oasis balls)

Cruel Tea for accessories that bring a little malice to tea time: *www.etsy.com*

Empty biodegradable tea bags: *www.amazon.co.uk*

Foil cupcake cases (for French Fancies recipe): *www.cakecraftshop.co.uk*

Glass teapots: *www.jingtea.com*

Good baking tins (including a perfectly straight-sided tin for French Fancies recipe): *www.utensa.co.uk*

Jam jars, pretty preserving bottles: *www.jamjarshop.com*

Kilner jars: *www.kilnerjar.co.uk*

Patterned chocolate transfer sheets: *www.mycakedecorating.co.uk*

Piping nozzles, food colouring pastes, cutters: *www.cakedecoratingstore.co.uk*

Taiyaki pans (for Taiyaki Cakes recipe): *www.japancentre.com* or *eBay*

Tea towel blanks: *www.thecleverbaggers.co.uk*

Wide drinking straws (for Bubble Tea recipe): *www.amazon.co.uk* or *eBay*

Great Addresses, Contacts and Blogs

Amazing chocolates contact:
Paul A Young (several branches in London).
www.paulayoung.co.uk

Bespoke tea dresses, fascinators and costumes contact:
Ruth Bennett (she is based in Wales but can do patterns via measurements).
www.therandomdressmaker.blogspot.co.uk

Chef James Benson's excellent and reasonably priced catering company based in Broadway in the Cotswolds.
www.bensonscateringltd.co.uk

Delicious cannoli:
Tony Cannoli at The Hungry Wolf Ltd, based in East London.
www.facebook.com/tonythetigerwolf

Jelly makers and extraordinary event creators:
www.bompasandparr.com

Superb cakes such as cupcakes, wedding cakes and French fancies:
Michelle Eshkeri of Lavender Bakery (based in Finchley, London; also delivers all over London).
www.lavenderbakery.co.uk

Temari cakes: Japanese baker Maki.
www.makiscakes.com

Emma Beddington: *www.belgianwaffling.com*

Helen Graves: *www.helengraves.co.uk*
Her blog on sandwiches: *londonreviewofsandwiches.wordpress.com*

James Benson: *www.thecotswoldfoodyear.com*

Lavender Bakery: *lavenderbakery.wordpress.com*

Madalene Bonvini-Hamel: *www.britishlarder.co.uk*

MsRiceanPeas (Karen Campbell): *www.kmcampbell.co.uk*

Regula Ysewijn: *www.missfoodwise.com*

Trish Deseine (expertise on chocolate): *www.trishdeseine.com*

Thanks

Firstly I'd like to thank the artist **Margaret Rodgers,** who happens also to be my mum, for her gorgeous witty drawings, and thanks also to my daughter **Sienna Rodgers** for help with styling photographs. A budding food stylist, she has an excellent eye for detail.

Thanks also to:

Michelle Eshkeri of Lavender Bakery for baking advice and testing recipes.

My testers: **Gwyneth Brock** of Vintage Afternoon Teas, **Ann Parsons** of the Secret Teapot, and **Catherine Phipps.**

Clare Embury of the wonderful florists Achillea Flowers in Mill Lane, West Hampstead, for location shoots.

Ali Cook of Bristol Vintage, for props.

Canon cameras for loan of the 6d camera.

My friend **Les Wong/Bellaphon** for loan of a tripod.

My neighbour **Karen Campbell** and her daughter **Lexi,** for eating much of the cake.

Thanks also to pest controllers (2 sets!) for finally getting rid of the mice that occurred afterwards #nightmare.

Gratitude also to my agent **Michael Alcock,** for his encouragement and optimism.

My editor **Caroline McArthur,** for commissioning this book.

Queries editor **Anne Sheasby,** who is a hard taskmistress, but from whom I learned a great deal.

Many, many thanks to designer **Doug Kerr.**

Thanks to all my guests who have come to my secret tea parties and my supper club, The Underground Restaurant.

Published by Square Peg 2014

2 4 6 8 10 9 7 5 3 1

First published in Great Britain in 2014 by
Square Peg
20 Vauxhall Bridge Road,
London SW1V 2SA

A Penguin Random House company

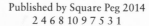

www.vintage-books.co.uk
www.penguinrandomhouse.com

A CIP catalogue record for this book is available from the British Library

ISBN 9780224098755

Photography: Kerstin Rodgers
Illustrations: Margaret Rodgers
Design: Well Made Studio

Penguin Random House supports the Forest Stewardship Council® (FSC®),
the leading international forest-certification organisation. Our books
carrying the FSC label are printed on FSC®-certified paper. FSC is the
only forest-certification scheme supported by the leading environmental
organisations, including Greenpeace.
Our paper procurement policy can be found at
www.randomhouse.co.uk/environment

Printed and bound in Germany by Mohn Media GmbH